LOST EMPIRES

THE PHENOMENON OF THEATRES
PAST, PRESENT AND FUTURE

Author's Note

Lost Empires drew on sources itemised in the Bibliography (page 160) and on the theatres' own internet sites and documentation. *The Theatres Trust Guide To British Theatres* was an invaluable map to a great past and a surviving present. *The Billy Rose Collection of the New York Public Library For The Performing Arts* was vital in assessing New York's great past and present.

Throughout the book I relied on the *Oxford Dictionary Of National Biography (DNB)*, and the *American National Biography (ANB)* for information. In the *DNB* these included these entries: Elizabeth Baigent on James Wyld; Tracy C. Davis on Sir Edward Moss; J.W. Ebsworth (revised Nilanjana Banerji) on Samuel Cowell; Richard Foulkes on William Macready; Kurt Gänzl on Emily Soldene; Frances Gray on Marie Lloyd; James Hogg on Dan Leno; W.J.Lawrence (revised J. Gilliland) on Lydia Thompson; Sara Maitland on Vesta Tilley; Javier Pes on Imre Kiralfy; Paul Ranger on Jonathan Tyers; Carole Rosen on Jenny Lind; Dave Russell on Thomas Barrasford, Joe Elvin, Sir Harry Lauder, Gilbert Hastings Macdermott, Charles Morton, Harry "Little Tich" Relph and Sir Oswald Stoll; Frank M. Scheide on Charlie Chaplin.

In the *ANB* there was: Mary C. Henderson on Charles Frohman; Tracy C. Davis on Maude Adams; Melissa Vickery-Bareford (and in the *DNB* Heidi J. Holder) on Ira Aldridge; Edward A. Berlin on Scott Joplin; Charles Hamm on Irving Berlin; Clair O. Haugen on Adah Isaacs Menken; Bruce A. McConachie on Edwin Forrest; James Ross Moore on P.T. Barnum and Tony Pastor.

Acknowledgements

If there had been no Hackney Empire, this book would never have been produced, and there would not have been a theatre had it not been for that group who, during the last two decades, have made it grow. There were many people, benefactors, builders and staff and to name names is invidious, but I will name a few of them anyway: Hazel Durrant, Colin Hilton, Louise Holmes, Sophie Medd, Claire and Roland Muldoon, Frank Sweeney and Simon Thomsett. Then there has been the (changing) board of directors, of whom I will mention just Ian Rushton, who resigned after chairing the board into a new era. And then there are the people of many other Empires and Imperials who have helped me.

For their encouragement and help I also thank Juliet Ash, John Fordham, Helen Mackintosh and Sheila Rowbotham. For encouragement, help — and (great) forbearance, many thanks to Monica Henriquez.

It was a comment from Colin Chambers that provided the initial idea for a book. It was the extraordinary insight and publishing flair of Gabrielle Mander at Cassell Illustrated which crystallized it, and made the book possible. It was Karen Dolan who edited it, Vickie Walters who provided the picture research and Simon Buchanan and Ron Callow at Design 23 who designed *Lost Empires*. They did so wonderfully.

And then, of course, there were the acts...

LOST EMPIRES

THE PHENOMENON OF THEATRES PAST, PRESENT AND FUTURE

NIGEL FOUNTAIN

CASSELL ILLUSTRATED

First published in Great Britain in 2005 by Cassell Illustrated,
a division of Octopus Publishing Group Limited
2-4 Heron Quays, London E14 4JP

Text copyright © 2005 Nigel Fountain
Design and layout copyright © 2005 Cassell Illustrated

A CIP catalogue for this book is available from the British Library.

ISBN 1 84403 345 7
EAN 9781844033454

Printed in China

Contents

Introduction

MY FIRST MEMORY of an Empire was fear. That came even before the excitement, the mystery, the trick of the light, the lustrous glow radiating off the stage. The show was a pantomime, that peculiar institution which still flourishes, half a century on, in British theatres every Christmas. The production was *Cinderella*.

That year my parents must have been broke. I was guided up stark, echoing staircases until we arrived in the cheapest seats, in the upper balcony. Not that it was explained to me like that. When pressed my parents could put a dramatic spin on fate. We were in the Gods, I was told, so named, they said, because we were so high up we were close to unknown, unseen deities.

The seats were steeply raked, and the stage so far below, and between me and that other reality was the void. I knew that, with one slip on those aisle steps, I would tumble into space, float into nothing, land — well, would I land at all?

I was, of course, being initiated into rituals with origins around flickering fires, shadows on cave walls, glints in animal eyes, blasted heaths and ancient myth. Wisely, nobody explained that to me, at the time. Maybe they were more concerned about getting away from family squabbles, ration books, bombsites, the world of postwar British austerity, because that velvet darkness, then, now, forever is excitement — and escape.

Once seated, I was safe, and stared down on poor but beautiful Cinderella sweeping the austere, albeit spacious castle kitchen. She was consoled only by her friend, the wise fool, Buttons. There was Baron Hardup fleeing from the Broker's Men, unkind behaviour from the Ugly Sisters, and Prince Charming's quest to find the foot which fitted the glass slipper.

But why was a baron, and thus a nobleman, poor? Why was Buttons, supposedly dumb, so smart? Why were the Ugly Sisters such peculiar-looking women? Why did Prince Charming have such fine legs? And come to that, was he a he at all? And were the sisters shes? From the Gods, for the five-year-old, it seemed a world turned upside down.

And indeed it was. Pantomime was an eighteenth-century British mutation from seeds scattered by touring Italian *commedia del arte* troupes. Their art, well, that in turn had origins in the Roman Empire's saturnalia, when the rich played poor, and the poor rich, sexes changed and things didn't fit. Wisely, nobody explained that to me at the time either.

Instead song and dance, jokes, absurdities, beauty, ugliness, pathos and farce were crammed into that building, the Empire, and I was left to my own devices, laughing at Buttons — played by Derek Roy, a then popular British radio comedian — lost in that space, one of those many strange places around

A lustrous glow and a vision out of Edwardian England. The Hackney Empire in the East End of London.

the world where people, having dreamed dreams, live them and draw others into them.

That Empire, my Empire, was in Southampton, the commercial seaport on England's south coast. Five days away on vastly expensive transatlantic liners like the *Queen Mary*, the *America*, the *Queen Elizabeth*, the *United States*, the *France* — was what was to me a mythical place, New York.

While I sat staring at Cinderella, some four thousand miles away on Broadway, Manhattan's last surviving theatre from the Victorian era, the

Empire, was still flourishing. It had been the creation of producer Charles Frohman, the "little, round, slant-eyed Buddha" who had grown rich in the days of King Edward VII and President Teddy Roosevelt, importing drama from London's West End on to the American stage.

But in 1915 Frohman had perished – he was a passenger on the torpedoed transatlantic liner *Lusitania* — en route to London and a meeting with *Peter Pan*'s creator JM Barrie. It was Frohman who in 1904 had encouraged Barrie to put the boy who wouldn't grow up on stage in London at the Duke Of York's Theatre. It was Frohman who had put *Peter Pan* on stage at the New York Empire in 1905. It was I, in the 1950s who, like a multitude of children before and since, benefited from Barrie and Frohman's efforts when I caught up with a touring *Peter Pan* myself, at that Southampton Empire. The play still carried the genes of that Edwardian production, with the incidental music still taken from a 1904 Broadway show, *Belle Of New York*.

When in 1915 Frohman died, he too had become a casualty in an Atlantic trade which already, at the time of his death, was more than a century old. From around the rim of that ocean, high art, song and dance, great drama, sleaze, high hopes, no-hopers and genius criss-crossed the seas on the way to the Saint John New Brunswick and Montreal Imperials, Baltimore and Saskatoon's Empires, Cape Town's Empire, a multitude of Empires dotted around Britain, not to mention Hippodromes, Royalties, Lyceums, Apollos, Comedys, Astors, Alexandras, Gaietys, Colonials, Palaces and all.

Four decades on from Frohman's death the fate of all those halls was at the mercy of technology, fashion, fate – and property developers. The theatre where I had seen that *Cinderella* was heading into rough times. It had opened in 1928, the last ever built for the then mighty Moss Empire variety circuit. In its early years Gracie Fields, Anna Pavlova, and Paul Robeson had played there, so had Stanley Holloway, who would be Albert Doolittle on Broadway in *My Fair Lady* a quarter of a century later. But in those years too Wall Street crashed, and Al Jolson sang on film.

By the mid-1930s the theatre was mainly a movie house. By the time I first set eyes on it, the Empire was almost invariably plying its trade as a cinema, and, matching that, was soon rechristened the Gaumont. Yet for years after, locals stuck to the old name, just as the theatre itself periodically reverted to its preferred profession as a variety house, putting on acts like Peter Sellers, Terry-Thomas and the Goons.

Then, in 1957 came a sign of the times. Jet airliners had started flying the Atlantic, but Bill Haley and his Comets, the balding, plaid-jacketed, middle-aged heralds for half a century of teen revolt, still docked by ocean liner at Southampton, and played to packed houses around Britain — and at the late Empire, Southampton. Grown-ups stayed home and watched their new televisions, but, in the reverberating old halls teenagers were sometimes replacing them, at rock 'n' roll shows.

But, with rock 'n' roll, Empires, as such, were surely past it. Hippodrome, Lyceum were vague words, anachronistic maybe, but they didn't carry any political charge. But Empire was a brand name that had been used when global real estate had been carved up in the nineteenth century, accompanied by a pageant of uniforms and plumes and panjandrums and howdahs and parades and twenty-one gun salutes. In that time, Empire theatres were part of the roar of applause around imperial pomp. Those music halls and variety theatres dotted not just the British landscape, but that of other pink parts of the world, British dominions and colonies like South Africa, India, Egypt, Singapore, Ceylon and Australasia, and the name extended to the United States as well. There were echoes from other colonial powers too, with their Imperials, from St Petersburg to Madrid, Paris to Naples.

But Empires were not fashion in the 1950s. They might still exist — as the Soviet Union and the United States — but those two powers were different. Marx and Coca Cola had replaced hope and glory. The British Empire was collapsing, its subjects were setting up for themselves, and the British themselves knew the game was over. The old empire theatres had resounded to tub-thumpers cheering up the imperial race — and most particularly a grumpy imperial working class —with stuff about distance and power:

> "Sons of the sea,
> All Britons born,
> Sailing every ocean,
> Laughing foes to scorn"

By the beginning of the 1950s such notions had vanished, there was no one serious to plug them anymore. Why there was even the character of Archie Rice, clapped-out variety comedian played by Laurence Olivier in John Osborne's 1957 play *The Entertainer*. In it Rice and a variety theatre ("Don't clap too hard. It's a very old building.") stood in for the British Empire — and indeed for Moss Empire theatres. As for the sons of the sea, the British singer

Petula Clark, who had begun as a child star in London variety theatres, had a big hit with a (German) song:

"Sailor,
Stop your roaming,
Come home,
Home to me"

As for me, I was soon to leave Southampton. Yet I was vaguely aware and vaguely unhappy too, that something was being written out of the vocabulary of the streets. In the late 1950s I had read in newspapers that Laurence Olivier's estranged wife, Vivien Leigh, Scarlett O'Hara herself, had led a north London protest march against the closure of one of London's most famous venues, Collins Music Hall in Islington Green. I was impressed, but puzzled. Just what was it they were so keen to protect?

After all, in Southampton, Empire-cum-Gaumont aside, there was only one other theatre, the once-sedate Grand. It was offering such shows as *Nude Follies* and, rather more imaginatively, I thought, *My Bare Lady*. It was following a familiar, if depressing path beaten (not that I knew it) by places like the nineteenth-century Empire Leicester Square in London, through Bowery burlesque in New York, to Hamburg's Reeperbahn dives, the Empire in Newark New Jersey — and Collin's itself in its last days.

I left Southampton soon after. But there was one last visit to the Empire-cum-Gaumont, and when I made it, I saw Ella Fitzgerald, Roy Eldridge and Coleman Hawkins. There was, I realised once more, a point to live acts. Ella wasn't a movie, she was there on stage, where *Cinderella* had been, and Eldridge and Hawkins were creating weird music, really weird music, much weirder than Bill Haley on the juke box, making it up, in front of me.

In the early 1960s a television journalist and writer Dan Farson, bought an inn on the Isle of Dogs in east London. It was called the Waterman's Arms. Farson was the son of an American reporter who had become famous for his wartime accounts of the Blitz from the capital. In making his purchase Farson had joined, in a small way, that old-established Atlantic trade in

An encounter on the Dogs: The Waterman's Arms where Dan Farson recreated a distant past, in the more recent past of the 1960s.

greasepaint. For what he was attempting to recreate, I heard then, was music hall, and I had begun to think about what Vivien Leigh had been trying to protect, and what was beginning to intrigue me — a Victorian Britain lost, back on the other side of the twentieth century. It was exciting.

It wasn't just me who felt this way. Fleetingly the Waterman's was a phenomenon; there was a live album recorded at the place; there were newspaper and television reports about the toff — American or no, Farson had the authentic, hesitant tones of an upper-class English education — and knees-ups down east. To me, before I got there, the pub seemed to have almost everything. It took in the lure of the big city, the exoticism of an east end, a lower east side, a Five Points of opium dens, rookeries and the romance of chancers and outlaws abandoning everything to do a flit in a tramp steamer on the morning tide. There, at the Waterman's, surely, was a door into a past.

It was the mid-1960s before I got to London, and to the Waterman's. By then Farson had quit — all I was ever to see of him was much later, as a figure sitting at the bar in a London Soho pub, the French's on Dean Street.

Today the Isle of Dogs is the location of Canary Wharf, a new capital of commerce; skyscrapers, chrome, flash, an electronic lymph gland of the global economy. That night, forty years ago it was a desolate place. The future of the local docks was then uncertain — extinction followed within two decades — the detritus of the Second World War persisted, there were some local council high-rise housing blocks under construction, there was poverty — there still is — and there was darkness. Getting down there meant a succession of trains and buses out of Hackney, across Mile End and down on to the Dogs. It was a pattern, I now realise, that was to recur, when in a different century, I began my quest for lost empires.

Finding the pub was not easy, it was near a church, down an alley, which ended on the banks of the River Thames, with blackness, silver glinting on the water. But just before that was the pub. Four decades on I remember the noise, the smoke, the laughter. I remember too, disappointment. It was not a music hall; it was a pub, a large pub true, but still a pub.

I had missed the point. It was out of tavern concerts and singing saloons that, in the mid-nineteenth century, music hall had grown, and to which, on that night, and on others, courtesy of Farson, it had retreated. What I was encountering were faint echoes, I guess, of what enticed people on New York's Bowery and London's Strand into the dives and cyder rooms — and pleasure gardens and music halls — in the first place.

I remember singing, bad jokes and noise, gold and scarlet, and, most of all, a huge black and white photograph of some star of the Edwardian music hall. A woman built, or at least fitted out, in the age of the *Dreadnought* battleship, with an hourglass figure, a pair of fine sturdy legs and an open smile. An icon, a survivor, Vesta Victoria.

I went back, but each time it got worse. By the mid–1960s, with the British Empire dead, there was a brief moment when its bric-a-brac became a fashion item, the stuff of Kaiser Bill's Batman, Granny Takes A Trip, and *Sergeant Pepper's Lonely Hearts Club Band*, The Beatles' allusion to the music hall and variety that had been part of their own Liverpool-Irish Atlantic rim childhood. But that spirit was short-lived. At the Waterman's the humour shrivelled into racism, a cancer that kills, and helped finally extinguish Farson's brave experiment.

But it did not kill my fascination with boards, halls, and empires. In the early 1970s, jobbing in journalism, I heard that, down in Wapping, in the London's East End there was an ancient music hall, recently rediscovered, and soon to be renovated by a "brave band of volunteers". Brave bands of volunteers go with the territory of the old theatres that have survived. Brave bands of volunteers, people who dream mad dreams, are a large part of what *Lost Empires* is about.

Wilton's Music Hall was not easy to find. It still isn't now, in times when car-friendly, people-hostile motor routes are raked through that tangled undergrowth of streets. Wilton's is in Wapping, set back from what, in the mid-nineteenth century was the horror of Ratcliffe Highway, a place of murder, robbery, prostitution, deprivation and degradation.

If the Waterman's, at best, was a mid-twentieth century sketch of an earlier time — evocative, sometimes wonderful —Wilton's, down Grace's Alley, *was* that time. There are places where one senses that the citizens of the egalitarian republic of the past have only just departed that space; maybe they left a second before. Not long before I got to Wilton's I had been in two thousand-year old Ephesus, in Asia Minor. One morning there, early, by a brothel and a library in fact, I had had that sensation. Mid-morning at Wilton's I had it too; there was the geography and sense of the nineteenth century on the streets, in the mind. Grey light filtered into a bar that had not served a drink then — things have changed in the intervening three decades — for more than ninety years. I wandered from room to room and into a main hall, with a tiny — by later standards — stage that, precisely because of the indifference of a century, seemed only just to have been vacated.

In London pasts are always there to be unveiled if you catch them, unaware, in back alleys, just above eye-level, on first floors — a faded street sign, a detail, an odd motif. At Wilton's that day I traced an 1840s route in my mind, when sailors came up from the Thames and the docks, through the stench of common conduits, through the shabby, urban chaos to what was, at first, just the Prince of Denmark public house. Soon a "concert room" had been added and there had been rooms to rent. In 1853 John Wilton turned it into a music hall and it was enlarged eight years later. Wilton's would have provided

JOHNNY FULLER. CAT IMPERSONATOR.

No hope or a whiskery living? Cat impersonator Johnny Fuller (*above*) and an old modern world, sex meets the bicycle.

entertainment, drink — and what amounted to a brothel too. It was a mid-nineteenth century palace of fun, a place to fleece seafarers of the money they had risked their lives to earn, a good business out of the control of the local authority, the government, Queen Victoria, a bit of the wild west down east, a primeval soup.

Wilton's survived two world wars, the Blitz, and repeated local redevelopments. The Greater London Council took it over in 1966 and it was eventually handed over to a trust. It has survived, and from that day in 1970 it became part of the terrain that reassured me about London. It was still there, history was lashed together, the ropes were still intact, frayed maybe, but there. I went in search of other such places, onetime homes of stars, no-hopers and ancient eroticisms. There weren't any, I thought. In the early 1970s there were still a lot of attractive old movie houses — some of which had once been theatres — being jostled by boutiques and department stores and record shops and amusement arcades and outstaying their welcome in London's West End. Soon they were all gone.

But soon after my visit to Wilton's, I was told about another mid-nineteenth century theatre, also down east, the Hoxton Hall, which flourished briefly as a music hall in the late 1860s. I dropped by. It was tiny and beautiful and there, maybe, I would have left it had it not been for a walk on a sunny afternoon in Hackney, a few years after my visits to Wilton's and the Hoxton Hall.

The Hackney Empire is not a place that passers-by miss. But Hackney

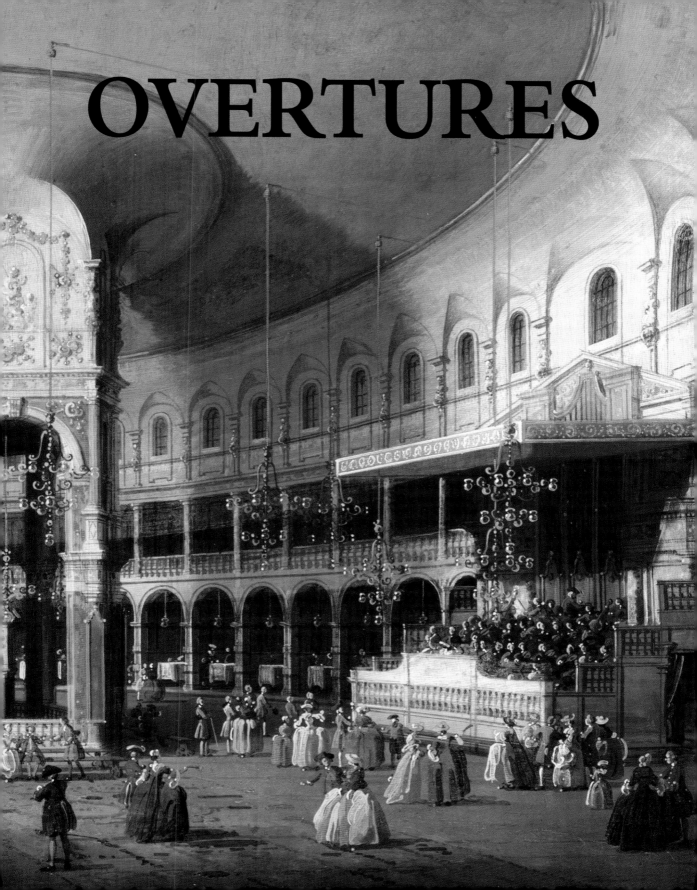

OVERTURES

Lost gardens

L ONG BEFORE VARIETY, vaudeville, music halls, Hippodromes, Alhambras and Empires there were travelling fairs, circuses, taverns, pantomimes, pleasure gardens and theatres. Since all were places of entertainment, all were also locations for real offstage — and onstage — battles. These battles echoed the art, they were about bawdiness and propriety, God and the Devil, the state and private enterprise, rich and poor, highbrow and lowbrow, young and old, natives and newcomers. And most of them ultimately blurred into tussles about land, money, and carving up real estate.

In the sixteenth century there were theatres east of the City of London, and a home for William Shakespeare, Kit Marlowe and others south of the City on the Surrey bank of the Thames. With the English Civil War, in 1642, the Puritans, having identified theatre as a tool of the King and of the rich,

Previous page: Keeping a sense of perspective? Inside at the Vauxhall Gardens.

When the going was good on the south side of the Thames. The Vauxhall Gardens in the early nineteenth century (*below and right*).

legislated it out of existence.

The stage reappeared in the 1660s with the restoration of King Charles II, and the licensing of "legitimate drama". The theatres that received royal patents were at Drury Lane and Covent Garden. But if there was to be legitimacy, there had to be illegitimacy; bootleg productions in non-patent theatres to be prosecuted on behalf of Drury Lane and Covent Garden.

In 1737 the Lord Chamberlain took over the licensing of theatres. There were only three theatres in London that could perform full-length plays — the Theatres Royal in Drury Lane and Covent Garden and the smaller Haymarket. Twenty-two years later came a move to regulate popular entertainment, Justices were to issue music and dance licences. Meanwhile the people of London continued to sing and dance, to watch illegitimate theatre — which could mean musically accompanied "dumb shows" and pantomimes — to get drunk and to fornicate.

The British had been joined at the theatre by those other subjects of the Empire across the Atlantic. And with the Americans came the opening act of the show that never closed, the entertainment trade around the Atlantic rim. In 1750 an English touring company performed

Richard III in New York's Nassau Street and in Williamsburg, Virginia. In New York in 1758 a theatre was opened at Crugers Wharf; three years later a theatre followed on Beekman Street New York. Six years after that another and more lasting venue — at least until the end of the eighteenth century — opened on John Street. Then came an interlude, the Revolutionary War when the John Street Theatre became the Theatre Royal and the main show in town was entertainment for the British occupying troops.

Then came the newly independent United States. With a population of just over 60,000 New York overtook Philadelphia as the largest city in the new country. And on January 29, 1798 the city got itself a new theatre, the Park, which opened on Park Row in Manhattan, a legitimate theatre to go with a multitude of saloons, and taverns — like the Bulls Head in the heart of the cattle-trading Bowery.

But by then London's population was approaching one million. It was the capital of a country waging a virtual world war with Napoleonic France. It was a cultural centre rivalling Paris. It had generated a host of famous actors — and by then actresses — a 300-year catalogue of drama, and an impressive array of public houses, hotels, theatres, brothels — and pleasure gardens.

Birds, and doggs, and hogs

"So I home and there find Creed also come to me. So there I spent much of the afternoon with them, and indeed she is a pretty black woman, her name Mrs. Horsely. But Lord! to see how my nature could not refrain from the temptation; but I must invite them to Foxhall, to Spring Gardens, though I had freshly received minutes of a great deale of extraordinary business. However I could not helpe it, but send them before with Creed, and I did some of my business; and so after them, and find them there, in an arbour, and had met with Mrs Pierce and some company with her. So here I spent 20s. upon them and were pretty merry. Among other things, had a fellow that imitated all manner of birds, and doggs, and hogs, with his voice, which was mighty pleasant. Staid here till night."

Samuel Pepys, May 29 1666.

SAMUEL PEPYS'S NIGHT out at Fox Hall was during that lull between the capital's two seventeenth century catastrophes. It was a year after the Great Plague, which had killed 70,000 Londoners out of a population not much above a quarter of a million. It was three months before the Great Fire, which was to devastate the city. But for Mrs Pepys, Mrs. Horsely, Mrs Pierce, Creed, and particularly the diarist, who was a frequent visitor, Spring Gardens, which had then been open just five years, had become part of the pleasure of London.

Londoners' ability to transform language soon transformed Fox (once Faulke) Hall into Vauxhall, The pleasures of London, as applied to Spring Gardens transformed them into what were described at the time as a "rural brothel". But then, in 1728, Jonathan Tyers bought the lease. The Gardens were transformed. He set out to return them, indeed enhance, their former glory. He was to prove himself a pioneer entertainment entrepreneur for London, and the world.

Within four years Tyers had completed initial reconstruction and established the New Spring Gardens at the centre of London society. At the 1732 "ridotto alfresco", admission was one guinea (105p), guests included the Prince of Wales and the gardens were open from 9pm until 4am.

Tyers cultivated the right people. There was music by Thomas and Michael Arne, an orchestra, a theatre in the rotunda and mock ruins — the Siege of Acre was a popular theme. William Hogarth provided paintings, and designed silver admission tickets; there were statues of John Milton and Frederick Handel — who visited the gardens with Mozart. There was a pavilion, bowers, waterfalls, an arcade, and at the end of the walks canvases — produced by Drury Lane theatre scene-painter Francis Hayman — offered vistas of classical and faraway places. Hayman also painted contemporary scenes for the Garden's alcoves.

Tyers knew how to make money. And he was a frugal mass caterer. Charles Dickens wrote a century later that the Gardens had been the "scene of secret and hidden experiments; that there, carvers were exercised in the mystic art of carving a moderate-sized ham into slices thin enough to pave the whole of the grounds".

Tyers's success inspired rivals. In 1742 Ranelagh Gardens was launched in Chelsea, flourished, but closed in 1805. In 1831 the Surrey Zoological gardens opened. Six years later, at Chelsea Reach, came the Cremorne Gardens. In the first half of the nineteeth century there were gardens around London, big and small, sometimes attached to taverns. There were gardens in Marylebone and Kings Cross, Bayswater and Highbury Barn, Clerkenwell and Rotherhithe — and gardens too in New York.

Pepys was followed to the Vauxhall Gardens by Fanny Burney, Beau Brummell, William Thackeray, Charles Dickens, rope tricks, circuses, novelty acts, doomed acts — a hermit in a false beard who told fortunes — and balloon ascents. But long before the 1850s the "quality" and the literati had been followed by decline, drunks, and fights, and the gardens were being eyed by property developers. In July 1859 the Royal Vauxhall Gardens, as the New Spring Gardens had become in 1831, staged a "farewell for ever" firework display and vanished. Entertainers meanwhile had gone on to the Crystal Palace, transplanted from Hyde Park to Sydenham — and to the music hall.

The Ranelagh Gardens in Chelsea opened in 1742, and closed in 1805, the year of Trafalgar.

There were gardens here

THREE HUNDRED AND thirty-nine years after Samuel Pepys's evening with his wife and Mrs Horsely, I follow him to where Spring Gardens should be. It is end-of-winter, with a cold west wind cutting down the Thames, under Vauxhall Bridge and towards the Houses of Parliament. The seventeenth-century prospect on the Surrey shore beyond Westminster was pastoral. In twenty-first century south London it is a see-through twelve-storey glass and brick high-rise and a 1960s spilt-coffee-colour office block with an HSBC bank, the headquarters of the London Fire and Emergency Planning Authority, and billboards for fully refurbished economic offices to let on flexible terms; no garden, just hard flat horizontals and verticals. Somewhere, across the river from the Tate Britain art gallery should be some hint of the garden.

I get to a finely mutilated late-Victorian public house. Down Tinworth Street, on the side of railway arches carrying South East Trains out of Waterloo are big, silver italics, Spring Gardens in fancy type. Beyond that, disappointingly, is a business park. "There were gardens here," I say to a security guard, "gardens, one hundred and fifty years ago." He looks at me like I am amiably mad. "I hadn't clocked in then," he says. We laugh.

All round me, is what replaced Jonathan Tyers's dream; sturdy small Victorian factories — Horatio Myers's splendid tiled bedstead manufacturers — and offices, long converted; the elevated railway track which cut the garden off from the river; post war council flats; two more Victorian pubs — one, the Vauxhall Bridge Tavern famous for its drag acts — and expanses of muddy grass bordered by Goding Street and New Spring Gardens Walk and Glasshouse Street and Topps Tiles and Majestic Wines and the Carpet Warehouse overshadowed by the riverside 1990s headquarters of MI6, spooks staring down on vanished revellers.

But across the grass, fronting on a cluster of semi-derelict mid-Victorian houses, is Spring Gardens City Farm. Where Samuel Pepys heard that fellow imitating birds, dogs, and pigs, and Charles Dickens watched a balloonist vanishing into the clouds, there are now cows, geese, horses, turkeys, rabbits, a brown goat and Vauxhall kids staring at the duck pond. It is wonderful, I say to two guys working at the farm. They agree. It got rough here towards the end, I add, back in the 1850s. It still is, replies one, gesturing out across the park. Two people got murdered here last week, out of the pub, after the entertainment.

I leave, past a horse in its paddock, and down into Tyers Street, the Dallas chicken bar and Payless Food and Wine and the traffic roar of Kennington Lane.

Heavy drinking, and sometimes a row

"Beer flowed freely: and it was about this time, at Cremorne, that the insidious 'long' drinks — soda and 'something' — now so popular, first made their appearance. Occasionally there were big banquets organised by certain "swells" and held there, when there would be heavy drinking, and sometimes a row — one Derby night, once, when there was a free fight, which lasted for hours, involving the complete smash of everything smasheable..."

EDMUND YATES REMEMBERING CHELSEA'S CREMORNE PLEASURE GARDENS IN THE 1840S.

DOWN BY THE wharf, the Thames is out, beyond glistening mud. There are the airliners making for Heathrow Airport, children's cries hanging in the air around Worlds End housing estate. Evening rush hour traffic, out of central London, pumps through Chelsea Embankment, Cremorne Road, into Edith Grove, on into Fulham and Putney and London's outer space.

Twenty-first century Cremorne Gardens is one of those spared, surprising green fragments of London. I have come to look at a relic.

The real Cremorne opened 170 years after the Vauxhall Gardens. It was cheaper than the Vauxhall and according to Edmund Yates, writing in the 1880s, it was better value and better laid out than its "very ghastly" rival. There was a weekly balloon ascent, a fine band, and a good dancing platform. Some grand old trees "afforded pleasant relief to town eyes which had been staring all day at brick and stucco". And there was ballet and fire-eating and performing animals too.

But the Cremorne also went into decline, just, coincidentally of course, as Chelsea was consolidating itself as an up-and-coming borough. That meant splendid new churches — and property developers. Pressure was on to push entertainment into variety theatres and dance halls or anywhere but not there, and as Yates wrote, "in our uncertain climate an open-air place of entertainment must always be a doubtful speculation".

Crucially, local pressure was on to curb prostitution, not a subject that Yates, writing in the 1880s — and fresh out of prison after a criminal libel conviction — would have touched on. Writing in 2004, drawing vividly on his grandmother's recollections of 1870s Chelsea, Donald James Wheal recreates a world of illicit prize-fighting amidst the Cremorne's elm trees, the gas-lit Fountain of Light, and a place where prostitution was the main

Gates into gaslight? The Cremorne Gardens' gates, surviving in the twenty-first century.

A question of aesthetics, and an issue of real estate. Whistler's *Nocturne In Black And Gold*, The Falling Rocket.

attraction, just as it was a key attraction in places of entertainment around London, whether the Pavilion in Whitechapel Road or the grand Empire in Leicester Square.

And then there were the fireworks over the Cremorne. Those illuminations became the subject, in 1877, of one Chelsea resident's art. The American James McNeil Whistler's *Nocturne In Black And Gold* led the critic John Ruskin to accuse him of "flinging a pot of paint in the public's face" and to the famous libel action between painter and critic.

That year the pressure from the middle classes finally did for the Cremorne. Its licence was withheld and it followed the other pleasure gardens into history, paved over, built-up, transformed into small factories and back-to-backs which survive today. Technology — steam and electricity — administered the coup de grace to the Vauxhall Gardens and the Cremorne. Vauxhall was cut off from its river by the railway, at the Cremorne, where in the 1840s steamboats had ferried customers back to Hungerford Bridge, the cauterisation was done by the grand, austere Lots Road power station and the London County Council water works, both themselves now doomed.

One thing remains, the relic for my evening in 2005. There had been some magnificent, 1830s eight-tonne sandblasted iron gates, apparently situated at the King's Road, Edith Grove entrance to the gardens. After they had gone, the gates went to a local brewery, Bowdens. By 1960 the brewery had become Watney Mann's and the new owners presented the gates to Chelsea council, whose predecessors had done for the gardens eighty years earlier. In 1981 the council restored the gates and in 1997 they were refurbished. Now they stand in isolation, in the middle of tiny Cremorne gardens, gravel and cobbles on one side, grass on the other, a scattering of flowers here and there, locked, Victorian, magnificent. Gates in surreal isolation, gates into gaslight.

INTERIOR OF CASTLE GARDEN, NEW YORK.

The pleasures of New York

In the early 1760s Samuel Fraunces, a probably white West Indian, opened the Mason's Arms on Upper Broadway in New York. Its success spurred him to open another tavern in 1763, the Queen Charlotte's Head — which soon became the Queen's Head — at Broad and Pearl Streets. It too was spectacularly successful. Two years after that Fraunces opened one of the first pleasure gardens in New York. The city already boasted a Spring Gardens; Fraunces's new enterprise was to be the Vauxhall, near where Greenwich and Thomas Streets now meet. That year too there was to be a Ranelagh at Church and Thomas Streets.

Fraunces enjoyed a spectacular career in New York and Philadelphia — including a spell as George Washington's household steward from 1789 to 1794 — but his Vauxhall was to vanish.

Its replacement came in 1804, with the opening of a new Vauxhall Gardens near Fourth

Atlantic transfer: After London, the gardens grew around the then Little Apple...

Avenue on land leased from John Jacob Astor. Just as in London there were garden walks, bowers for ladies, and chairs under the trees where men could smoke and drink. Unlike its London equivalent, it was used a lot in daytime. Like its London equivalent there was space for performances, in this case a large wooden shed, used for itinerant acting troupes, for dances, and for that entertainment staple, firework displays.

But in 1825 the lease expired, and Astor built Lafayette Place straight through the gardens. Within five years the Vauxhall's popularity had faded, as the smart trade headed for the new Niblo's Garden on Broadway and Prince Street, but then, in 1840, along came Phineas Taylor Barnum...

African-Americans were refused admission to the New York's Vauxhall Gardens. Any black customer at the Park Theatre was sent to a segregated area. Such rules did not apply at William Henry Brown's tiny garden at 38 Thomas Street. The African Grove was a black venue. Brown, a West Indian who had worked as a steward on the New York to Liverpool packet boats, sold beer, spirits, cakes and ice cream to a community under permanent siege. He also provided music, based around drums and clarinets. Complaints from the neighbours led him to shift the show indoors that autumn, into what Brown at first called the African

27

Ira Aldridge.

Theater — later the American Theater — offering music, comedy and Shakespeare and getting a black, and white, audience. Brown's business was booming and he moved it to Mercer and Bleeker Street, and then later to premises next to the city's most prestigious theatre, the Park. The Park responded by hiring thugs to drive away the competition and Brown retreated to Bleeker Street. There he and his performers survived an attack by a Canal Street circus troupe, but sometime in mid-1823 his show vanished, and with it, for many years, black theatre in New York City.

Amongst the performers at Brown's American Theater on Bleeker and Mercer Street was an African-American teenager. Ira Aldridge, the son of a minister — who disapproved of his son's acting ambitions — was

still studying at New York's African Free School. The closing of Brown's theatre in 1823 underlined the bleakness of job prospects in the United States for a black actor. So he got a job as a dresser with the London actor Henry Wallack, and in 1824 Aldridge sailed for Liverpool with the actor's brother.

In October 1825 as "Mr Keene" he made his London stage debut in a "grand West Indian melodrama" *The Revolt Of Surinam*, as the royal slave Oroonooko, at the Royal Coburg Theatre near Pimlico — and was rewarded with a racist review in *The Times*. He subsequently toured the north, Scotland and Northern Ireland and played London's East End, in white, as well as black roles. He made his West End debut as Othello at the Theatre Royal Covent Garden — the audiences were warm but racism pervaded the critics' response, and resumed provincial tours. Then, in the early 1850s, he began working in continental Europe. His success in Switzerland, Germany, Russia, and Austria-Hungary, he received a string of honours, fed back into his work in England. By 1858 the critics had changed their tone and five years later he became a British citizen. He died in 1867, aged 60.

If he was to be believed, among the audience at one of the young Ira's early performances at the African Theatre was a jobbing English actor, Charles Mathews, who, back home, had specialised in comic north country routines. Dropping by in Bleeker Street, he saw Ira singing and incorporated the song into his new show, *A Trip To America*, which featured a Yankee character, and a black character. It was one of the earliest examples of "blackface" minstrelsy, the racist depiction of blacks by whites — and sometimes blacks — which was to be a key part of music hall and variety for more than a century, and would survive on British television into the 1970s.

Blending healthful and moral instruction with recreation

"Looking back on a long and eventful career, I confess in no boasting vein that I have conscientiously laboured to elevate and ennoble public amusements, which play no small part among the educational agencies of the times. How successful I have been in blending healthful and moral instruction with recreation, it is not for me to state, but the satisfaction experienced in my life-work has been in itself a reward altogether apart from and superior to any golden harvest I may have reaped. Not that I am insensible to the latter...

FROM A LETTER FROM P.T. BARNUM TO THE REVEREND E.H.CAPEN, READ AT TUFTS COLLEGE ON JUNE 18, 1884.

Small star, big money: Barnum and Tom Thumb.

IN HIS LIFETIME more than one million copies of his constantly revised autobiography were published; more than forty-one million people paid twenty-five cents — half-price for children — to visit his twice-burned down "American Museum" in New York City; he lured Jenny Lind, the "Swedish Nightingale" to the United States in 1850 for a tour which opened up the transatlantic trade to a new age of celebrity show business, and in 1882 lured mighty seven-ton Jumbo the elephant from the London Zoo into a life of US show business.

Long before most impresarios had done anything, Phineas Taylor Barnum, the showman from Bethel Connecticut, born in 1810, died in 1891, had done pretty well everything, and mixed media before there was media to mix. Into a new world of industry, meagre education, boundless curiosity, quack science and a raging demand for entertainment, Barnum launched a (short-lived) crusading newspaper, a (bogus) "Feejee Mermaid",

George Washington's (bogus) 134-year-old nurse, the first hippopotamus to tour the US, and his own lectures on "go-aheaditiveness".

The US was entranced by the "English General", two-foot tall Charles S Stratton, promoted by Barnum as Tom Thumb, just as the British — and Queen Victoria — were captivated by the "American General", that same Tom Thumb. Barnum offered, at the American Museum, a new and wildly successful form of theatre, which took in live shows, lectures, and novelty acts. Through a succession of fairs-cum-circuses, on the road, and in the imagination, he defined and proclaimed the Greatest Show On Earth.

A little stage-struck neighbourhood

The proprietor of a private theatre may be an ex-scene painter, a low coffee-house keeper, a disappointed eighth-rate actor, a retired smuggler, or uncertificated bankrupt. The theatre itself may be in Catherine Street Strand, Strand, the purlieus of the city, the neighbourhood of Gray'-Inn lane, or the vicinity of Sadler's Wells; or it may, perhaps, form the chief nuisance of some shabby street, on the Surrey side of Waterloo-bridge.

The lady performers pay nothing for their characters, and it is needless to add, are usually selected from one class of society; the audiences are necessarily of much the same character as the performers, who receive, in return for their contributions to the management, tickets to the amount of money they pay. All the minor theatres in London, especially the lowest, constitute the centre of a little stage-struck neighbourhood.

CHARLES DICKENS, ON THE PRIVATE THEATRES OF LONDON IN THE 1830S.

AT THE TIME of the Battle of Waterloo in 1815, London theatre was booming. True, both the Theatre Royals, in Drury Lane and Covent Garden, had burned down in 1808-1809, but they were rebuilt. At Covent Garden the management tried to hike prices in an attempt to focus on the "quality" audience but all they provoked was a two-month protest, after which they backed down. As for their theatrical rivals, since they couldn't put on full-length plays, they offered burlettas, which mixed music and verse — and were far more popular than most straight plays — and the raw material of what would be reborn within forty years in music hall, song and dance, clowns, circus and pantomimes.

Fluctuations aside, growth continued into mid-century and the era of London's Great Exhibition of 1851, just as the demography of New York and London exploded. In 1810 the population of the five boroughs that would make up New York City was 119,734. By 1830 it was 242, 278. New York might still be provincial by the standards of great European cities but a flood of immigration was transforming it. As for greater London, by 1830 there were two and a quarter million souls within it. Twenty years later the population of the borough of Manhattan was past half a million.

Industrialism transformed theatre technology. In 1817 gaslight was used on stage for the first time in London. By 1820 both Drury Lane and Covent Garden had replaced candle and oil lighting with gas. When the glittering New York Theatre opened in 1826, one of its features was gas-illuminated globe lighting. Twelve years later Charles Kean, son of Edmund and the leading British actor of the mid-Victorian era, began using limelight in London theatres. Lime, combusting in a gas jet, could focus a white beam on a performer — thus providing a fresh boost to the evolving system of stardom, better special effects — and greater opportunities for theatres to burn down. It was Kean too who, in 1848, introduced the electric carbon arc light to the London stage.

Combined with the growing size of some

theatres, the outline of a mass medium was taking shape, a medium on which another developing mass medium, newspapers, penny papers as dominant literary forms, could focus, whether they were reviewing or running with scandal and controversy, like the 1849 events at New York's Astor Place.

But technology and new stars aside, show business for most Londoners and New Yorkers was the stuff of pleasure gardens, the private theatres that Dickens was writing about, the horrors of the "penny gaffs", tavern saloons — and song and supper rooms.

A defining moment in London came with the 1843 Theatres Act, which removed the unique status of Covent Garden and Drury Lane — thus opening up theatre to anyone with a licence from the Lord Chamberlain. That had been preceded in 1840 by a straw in the wind, the battle around Sam Lane's Union Saloon in Shoreditch, east London.

For offering song, supper and theatre, Lane was prosecuted and fined. He responded by leading a march on the Houses of Parliament. His slogans were "Workers want theatres" and "Freedom for the people's amusements".

The 1843 Act's stipulations were confusing — just what amounted to refreshments? — but the effects were long-lasting. The Act provided the seedbed out of which music hall theatre would grow. It meant that some tavern saloons became licensed theatres, while other venues clung to their drinks licences; this meant that they could not stage full-length plays. Instead they offered song and dance, recitations,

comedy routines, and that prototype of the nude show, the *poses plastiques.*

In New York six years later the physical battle around the Astor Place Opera House defined a new era in American theatre, for whites at least, since blacks were largely barred from such places. Opera was for the upper classes and the upper middle classes — as it was in London. Melodrama attracted the middle classes to theatre, while the working classes, and young middle class took in variety at concert saloons.

In the first half of the nineteenth century New York entertainment began to solidify around Park Row — location of the Park Theatre — on Broadway at City Hall and Houston, on West Broadway and on the Lower Bowery. That was where the New York Theatre opened in 1826 on the site of the Bulls Head Tavern, in what had been the centre of the abattoir area of Manhattan. It soon changed its name to the Bowery. "The Park Theatre is the only one licensed by fashion,' wrote the sceptical English visitor Fanny Trollope in 1830, "but the Bowery is infinitely superior in beauty; it is indeed as pretty a theatre as I ever entered, perfect as to size and proportion, elegantly decorated, and the scenery and machinery equal to anything in London, but it is not the fashion."

Indeed it wasn't. And it was on New York that Trollope centred her compliments, and even there she had strong words for the behaviour of American audiences. At the Chatham Theatre she "observed in the front row of a dress-box a lady performing the most maternal office

To the unintroduced traveller from the Old World our city offered but few attractions. It was unhesitatingly pronounced dull by the English sporting gentleman, "horrible" by the Parisian who revelled in the ever changing pleasures of the gay Capital."

ABRAM C DAYTON, RECALLING FROM THE 1870S, THE NEW YORK OF THE 1830S.

Legitimate as they come: The Theatre Royal Drury Lane, early in the nineteenth century.

possible; several gentlemen without their coats, and a general air of contempt for the decencies of life, certainly more than usually revolting".

But it was worse in Cincinnati: There "the spitting was incessant" amidst a "mixed smell of onions and whiskey" and the "bearing and attitudes of the men are perfectly indescribable; the heels thrown higher than the head, the entire rear of the person presented to the audience, the whole length supported on the benches". The noise was perpetual, "and of the most unpleasant kind; the applause is expressed by cries and thumping with the feet, instead of clapping; and when a patriotic fit seized them and 'Yankee Doodle' was called for, every man seemed to think his reputation as a citizen depended on the noise he made."

But then Fanny Trollope was a lady, and as such, she would have kept well away from places like Sadlers Wells Theatre in Islington, London, described ten years after her Cincinnati experiences as providing a "bear garden, resounding with foul language, oaths, catcall shrieks, yells, blasphemy, obscenity — a truly diabolical clamour".

Even the Drury Lane Theatre in 1849, wrote Clement Scott, provided very little luxury. The pit was right up to the orchestra and the "faithful pittites sitting on hard benches" were "constantly disturbed between the acts by women with huge and clumsy buckets filled with apples, oranges, nuts, ginger beer bottles, stout and bills of play."

A desire for welsh-rabbits

Going to the play then, and to the pit, as was the fashion in those merry days, with some young fellows of my own age, having listened delighted to the most cheerful and brilliant of operas and laughed enthusiastically at the farce, we became naturally hungry at twelve o'clock at night, and a desire for welsh-rabbits and good old glee-singing led us to the 'Cave of Harmony'.

WILLIAM THACKERAY'S NOVEL *THE NEWCOMES*, 1854.

ONE NIGHT IN the late-1960s I visited one of those clubs that, in that psychedelic era, germinated, bloomed, and withered. The Perfumed Garden was briefly in King Street, bordering on Covent Garden Piazza. It was in the basement of an old warehouse, in that time when the fruit market was beginning its retreat from central London to a new home south of the River Thames, west of Vauxhall Bridge.

What I found at 43 King Street then was an old, vaguely intriguing basement. But number 43 had a history to which, on that night I was completely indifferent, since its excitement then was that of those times, love generations, drugs and Soft Machine. But the youth in that basement, that night, were the latest of at least six generations searching for, and sometimes finding, a big night out in Covent Garden.

Thackeray's Cave Of Harmony was an amalgam of at least three places. In 1773 at 43 King Street there was a tavern run by a Mr Joy. Taken over by a W.C. Evans it became Evans (Late Joys) and the basement became a song and supper club. It was further developed in the 1840s by John "Paddy" Green, a sometime chorus singer at the Adelphi Theatre. Next door to Evans was Gliddon's Divan, a tobacconist-cum-smoking room, popular with young swells, soon to be replaced by an "American bowling alley".

A few hundred yards away in Maiden Lane there was another song and supper club, the Cyder Cellars. To complete that triangle of Victorian popular culture, in nearby Fountain Court, across the Strand, was the Coal Hole.

Within those three venues, within ten minutes walk of each other, seeds of music hall were sown, even if, in some cases, their crop was ruthlessly pruned. Evans in the 1840s, during its ribald years, wrote Edmund Yates, had a good reputation for music, including a Herr von Joel, "who sang jodling ditties, played tunes on what he called a "vokingshteeck" and gave capital imitations of the birds and beasts of a farmyard". And there was comic vocalist J.W. Sharpe, who played the Vauxhall and Cremorne pleasure gardens in the summer, but was always to be playing Evans's "for a guinea a week and supper each night", until drink got him, and he was found dead, from starvation, on a country road.

But by the mid-1850s music hall was emerging and Evans's song and supper attempted to ride the wave of the future. Green had the garden covered over, and the basement where Sharpe had sung his songs became a vestibule-cum-annexe, hung with pictures — an important feature of early music hall — where the (male) clientele could meet next to the concert room, which now featured a stage. There was also a supper room. "Chops and potatoes — never to be equalled — were the ordinary supper," wrote Yates. Between 1858 and 1860 "some of the smartest talk in London was to be heard" he added, "when the old night clubs had ceased to be, and the present ones had not been thought of." Crucially women were admitted to the gallery, where they could see, without being seen. But they had to give their names and at Evans competition from the music halls — where "respectable" women were in the years ahead to make up a large part of the audience — spelt the end of Green's success.

Evans's Song and Supper Club.

Men dressed up in women's clothes

A jury was selected; the prosecutor opened his case, which to suit the depraved taste of the patrons, was invariably one of seduction or crim.con. (adultery). Witnesses were examined and cross-examined, the females being men dressed up in women's clothes, and everything was done that could pander to the lowest propensities of depraved humanity.

J. EWING RITCHIE RECALLING A NIGHT AT THE JUDGE AND JURY SOCIETY AT THE GARRICK'S HEAD, BOW STREET IN THE 1840S.

RENTON NICHOLSON WAS thirty-two when in 1841 he set up, and starred in, the Judge and Jury Society at the Garrick's Head, a large tavern opposite the Covent Garden theatre. The Society was an instant success for a man Yates described as "clever, versatile, wholly unprincipled" and the sometime editor of "an atrociously blackguard weekly journal called *The Town*".

As the judge Nicholson presided over an improvised parody of British justice — which developed, for a time, a following amongst lawyers, politicians and the aristocracy, so much so that the "jury" at the shows was often made up of real MPs and peers. He took the show on the road, to the Cremorne Pleasure Gardens, to southern race meetings, and, preceded by the Victorian equivalent of a media blitz, to provincial towns like Southampton.

Nicholson's career was a model for the next one hundred and fifty years of show business chancers. Stage aside, his career took in billiard hustling, card sharping, a time in prison as a debtor, destitution, speeling — race course roulette — the editing of two gossip rags, and pulp books on boxing.

There were plenty of *improvisatore* around during Nicholson's heyday; performers who, with echoes in the work of twenty-first century comedians and rappers, relied on audiences to

spark off improvised poems, jokes, and songs. The "Lord Chief Baron" offered a complete show, plus the pseudo-nudity of *poses plastiques* and *tableaux vivants*, and it was one that survived from the mid-1840s to the 1860s. In that time the Society ducked and dived from the Garrick's Head, to the Coal Hole in the Strand, the Justice Tavern in Bow Street and finally, in 1858, the Cyder Cellar in Maiden Lane. Three years later Nicholson died.

The likes of Renton Nicholson would become a staple of British and North American stage, not to mention stage, screen, television and tabloid, but in those days Covent Garden's nightlife was changing. As the 1850s progressed "ribaldry" receded. Acts cleaned up, or faced a greater threat from the music hall. The Coal Hole meanwhile was known, wrote Edmund Yates, for "a dreadful old creature called Joe Wells, who used to sing the most disgusting ditties".

It was a theme famously covered by Thackeray in his novel *The Newcomes*, when Colonel Newcome, back from the colonies, visits the "Cave Of Harmony" with his son. There they encounter the elderly Captain Costigan, "a gentleman in a military frockcoat and duck trousers of a dubious hue" who after a whisky-and-water, leering, with a "horrid grin" selects "one of the most outrageous

The entertainment was undoubtedly clever, but was so full of grossness and indecency,
expressed and implied, to render it wholly disgusting.

EDMUND YATES ON THE JUDGE AND JURY SOCIETY.

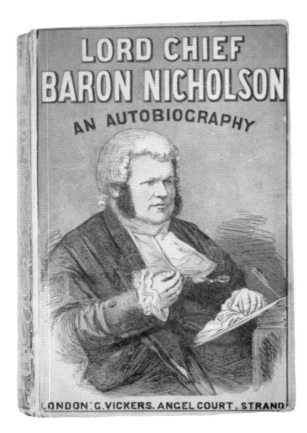

After the show, the kiss-and-tell: the cover of the memoirs of the "Lord Chief Baron" Renton Nicholson.

" 'Go on!' cries the Colonel in his high voice, trembling with anger. 'Does any gentleman say "Go on?" Does any man who has a wife and sisters, or children at home, say "Go on" to such disgusting ribaldry as this? Do you dare, sir, to call yourself a gentleman, and to say that you hold the king's commission, and to sit down amongst Christians and men of honour, and defile the ears of young boys with this wicked balderdash?'

" 'Why do you bring young boys here, old boy?' cries a voice of the malcontents.

" 'Why? Because I thought I was coming to a society of gentlemen, cried out the indignant Colonel. 'Because I never could have believed that Englishmen could meet together and allow a man, and an old man, to disgrace himself. For shame on you, old wretch! Go home to your bed, you hoary old sinner! And for my part, I'm not sorry that my son should see, for once in his life, to what shame and degradation and dishonour drunkenness and whisky may bring a man. Never mind the change sir! — Curse the change!' says the Colonel, facing the amazed waiter. 'Keep it until you see me in this place again; which will be never by George, never!' And shouldering his stick, and scowling around at the company of scared bacchanalians the indigent gentleman stalked away, his boy after him."

performances of his *répertoire*, and fires off a "tipsy howl by way of overture".

"At the end of the second verse the Colonel started up, clapping on his hat, seizing his stick, and looking as ferocious as if he was going to do battle with a Pindaree. 'Silence!' he roared out.

" 'Hear, hear!' cried certain wags at a farther table. 'Go on Costigan!' said others.

Come ye from the East, the West, North or the South,
Look in on the Baron, and wash out your mouth.

FROM AN EARLY HANDBILL FOR "LORD CHIEF BARON"
RENTON NICHOLSON'S JUDGE AND JURY SOCIETY.

The filthiest sayings

Here the stage, instead of being the means for illustrating a moral precept, is turned into a platform to teach the cruelest debauchery. The audience is usually composed of children so young, that these dens become the school-rooms where the guiding morals of a life are picked up; and so precocious are the little things, that the girl of nine will, from constant attendance at such places, have learnt to understand the filthiest sayings, and learnt to laugh at them as loudly as the grown-up lads around her.

THE JOURNALIST HENRY MAYHEW AT A "PENNY GAFF" IN THE LATE 1840s.

WHEN MAYHEW VISITED that penny gaff in London's Smithfield in the late 1840s he was mingling in a section of society where an almost free, certainly impoverished, market obtained in entertainment. For the costermongers that Mayhew interviewed home had few attractions. They were people "whose life is a street-life", far better the "conversation, warmth, and merriment of the beer-shop" — and until 1839 there were no restrictions on London public houses' opening hours. Even after that limitations were few. Alternatives, or supplements to pubs included rat-killing, dogfights, boxing, theatre — and the gaffs.

Admission, wrote Mayhew was a penny. The venues were shops transformed into temporary theatres, and at Smithfield, chosen, added Mayhew, because it was one of the "least offensive", the crowd had been attracted by a band playing dance tunes.

As for the show, there was a dancing fourteen-year-old girl, and a "funny gentleman" sang a song. The point of this, said Mayhew, "consisted in the mere utterance of some filthy word at the end of each stanza. Nothing however could have been more successful. The lads stamped their feet with delight; the girls screamed with enjoyment."

The last scene, "perfect in its wickedness"

Before the admen got in on the act: Early nineteenth-century entertainment advertising.

was a ballet between a "man dressed up as a woman, and a country clown. The most disgusting acts were struck, the most immoral acts represented, without one dissenting voice."

And the audience? Most of the two hundred in the gaff were women and girls, there were around thirty boys and eighteen men. "Forward they came, bringing an overpowering stench with them, laughing and yelling as they pushed their way through the waiting room. One woman carrying a sickly child with a bulging forehead was reeling drunk, the saliva running down her mouth as she stared about her with a heavy fixed eye. Two boys were pushing her from side to side, while the poor infant slept, breathing heavily, as if stupefied, through the din. Lads jumping on girls' shoulders, and girls laughing hysterically from being tickled by the youths behind them, every one shouting and jumping, presented a mad scene of frightful enjoyment."

Clearly something had to change in the entertainment business. But not too fast, as the Sam Hall mania indicated.

Oh, me name it is Sam Hall, chimney sweep,
  chimney sweep,
Oh, me name it is Sam Hall, chimney sweep;
Oh, me name it is Sam Hall, and I rob both great
  and small,
And me neck will pay for all when I die, when I die,
And me neck will pay for all when I die,
Damn their eyes
Excerpted from 'The Ballad Of Sam Hall'

In the late 1840s, the announcement that W.G. Ross was to sing the ballad at the Cyder Cellars in Covent Garden ensured the place would be packed out. To this day the darkness of the Victorian underworld still seeps from that recited song about the murderous, unforgiving, unforgiven chimney sweep. For me it still

generates the slow-motion horror of nightmares.

Legs akimbo, back to front on a chair, elbows resting on its back, Ross, unshaven, dressed and looked the part. The song itself had already been around for more than a century in various forms, focused on Captain Kydd, and Jack Hall, who had been hanged at Tyburn in 1707. It was Ross who revised the lyrics and provided the chilling rendition one hundred and forty years later.

Born in Glasgow, a sometime compositor, Ross built his career at the Cyder Cellars with songs like Pat's Leather Breeches and The Lively Flea. Then came Sam Hall.

But there were to be no more great successes. When the good times at the Cellars drew to a close, he did take the show on the road, and portraits of Ross as the killer sweep fetched a shilling at the halls where he played. But twenty years later the man who had made a living out of a criminal psychopath was playing Father Christmas in a south London pantomime. His career seems have concluded in the chorus at the Gaiety in London's West End which was probably more cheerful than the conclusion to the career of Sam Cowell.

Not long ago in Vestminster,
There lived a Ratcatcher's Daughter,
But she didn't quite live in Vestminster,
For she lived t'other side of the vater.
Her father caught rats, and she cried Sprats,
All about and over the quarter;
And the gentlefolk, they all bought their sprats,
Of the pretty little Ratcatcher's daughter.
Excerpted from 'The Ratcatcher's Daughter'

In the 1850s Cowell had a huge, if now baffling, hit, with 'The Ratcatcher's Daughter', written by Cuthbert Bede, "Verdant Green the

A talent for mimicry: Sam Cowell, big in England, big in America,
burned-out in Blandford.

Oxford Freshman", otherwise known as the Reverend Edward Bradley. Its success underlined Cowell's emergence as one of the first great, and doomed, stars of the new music hall.

There were other songs that Cowell made famous too, notably 'Clara Cline', 'Black Your Boots', 'Billy Barlow' and another tune which enthralled the London of the Great Exhibition era, 'Villikins And His Dinah'. The latter was not Cowell's song. It had originally been sung by Frederick Robson in one of London's most famous saloon theatres, the Eagle public house's Grecian Saloon off City Road in 1844.

Cowell's status was confirmed when he opened Charles Morton's new Canterbury Music Hall, in 1852. He was booked into Morton's next enterprise, the Oxford in Tottenham Court Road before it was built.

The son of a distinguished actor, Cowell had an actor's range, a powerful voice and a talent for mimicry. Like Harry Lauder, he would preface verses with witty, critical asides about the song's developing plot.

Born in London in 1820, he was taken by his father to the United States two years later and educated at a military academy near Philadelphia. Aged nine, he debuted on stage in Boston, singing a duet with his father. After that

In the darkness of Victorian England: W.G. Ross as the mythical, murderous, Sam Hall.

he played every major American theatre. Then came four years in Edinburgh before he based himself in London and moved away from acting towards comedy entertainment.

Cowell played the Cremorne and Vauxhall pleasure gardens, he was central to the success of Evans's supper rooms — and even made two appearances before Queen Victoria at Windsor Castle.

At the end of the 1850s, after a successful British tour, Cowell returned to the United States. That tour broke his health, and he apparently developed tuberculosis. Back in London he was invited to recuperate in Blandford, by a friend, the landlord of the Crown public house. The arrival of Cowell in the town, a ghostly and pale figure, caused a sensation. He consumed a bottle of brandy a day, it was said — when he could get it. "Safe! Safe!" he said on March 11, 1864 — and died. Funds were raised for his wife and children, and he was buried on the edge of the little Dorset town. "Here," says the inscription, "lies all that is mortal of Sam Cowell." He was 43.

Five months later Robson, the man who had launched 'Villikins And His Dinah' died of drink. He was 43.

THE RATCATCHER'S DAUGHTER

WITH EXTRA VERSES BY CHARLES SLOMAN,

THE MUSIC COMPOSED AND SUNG BY

SAM. COWELL.

The Musical Treasury, No. 749-50.

Ent. Stat. Hall.—Price Sixpence.

LONDON: DAVIDSON, 19 PETER'S HILL, DOCTORS' COMMONS.

Mysteries of the past: 'The Ratcatcher's Daughter' was a smash hit of the 1850s.

The dawn of a new time, the Oxford Music Hall in the mid-nineteenth century (*above*); Charles Morton, 'Father Of The Music Hall' caricatured (*right*).

Pipes and porter

The room is crowded, and almost every gentleman has a pipe or cigar in his mouth. Evidently the majority present are respectable mechanics or small tradesmen with their wives and daughters and sweethearts. Now and then you see a midshipman, or a few fast clerks and warehousemen. Everyone is smoking, and everyone has a glass before him; but the class that comes here are economical, and chiefly confine themselves to pipes and porter.

J.E. RITCHIE ON AN 1857 VISIT TO THE CANTERBURY MUSIC HALL.

IN THE EARLY 1830s, Charles Morton, just entering his teens, paid his first visit to a theatre. Run by Isaac Cohen, the Pavilion, the "Drury Lane of the East" attracted a Jewish audience and sailors from the nearby London docks. It offered melodramas and adventures like *A Wreck Ashore*, *The Lost Ship*, *The Mutiny At The Nore*, *Black-Eyed Susan*. It was the stuff of the low-brow popular entertainment that featured from London to New Orleans. Morton, a Hackney kid, ranged out across East End saloons and theatres, places like the Garrick in Whitechapel. The pattern of his career was being set.

By the 1840s Morton had moved west across London and married. He was running the St George's Tavern in Belgrave Road, Pimlico, a pub with a "sporting" reputation — Morton was a bookmaker on the side — patronised by staff from Buckingham Palace, just ten minutes walk away. Indeed it was said that Morton dropped by the Palace to dine with the cooks.

Morton also started a men-only "free and easy" in the pub's concert room. It was still that time when the women who patronised such places were either "daughters of joy", prostitutes, or assumed to be. Morton moved on to the Crown in Pentonville, north London, and, after five years, to the India House in Leadenhall Street in the City of London. But Morton had other plans, and they were not ones that could be developed in an area like the City.

Morton had seen the success of Covent Garden venues like Evans's song and supper room. In the wake of the 1843 Theatre Act the transformation in entertainment had begun. On Drury Lane the Mogul Saloon — where the New London Theatre now stands — opened just after Christmas in 1847. The following year the Grand Harmonic Hall at the Grapes Tavern on Southwark Bridge Road became the Surrey Music Hall. It was one of the first times that the term music hall had been attached to a venue. There were similar developments outside London. What Morton was about to do was not unique, but he was a pioneer — and a great publicist. The final seal of approval would come forty years later when he was proclaimed, "Father of the Halls" by the *Daily Telegraph's* drama critic Clement Scott.

On the south side of the river in Lambeth,

THE JUVENILE PROFESSORS OF THE TRAPEZE AT THE OXFORD MUSIC HALL.

Short legs come in handy: a mid-nineteenth century trapeze artist (*above*);
Charles Morton's Canterbury Hall goes advertising itself (*right*).

not far from the Royal Vauxhall pleasure gardens were the Lambeth Marshes, close to the Thames, prone to flooding, and regarded as a semi-criminal slum. There, in the 1840s, in Upper Marsh, off Westminster Bridge Road, was the Canterbury Arms. It was a pub with two bars, a bowling green and a club room. In December 1849, a year after the opening of the nearby Waterloo railway station, Morton took over the Canterbury. He began holding free and easies on Mondays and Saturdays. Then, and crucially, he introduced a "ladies' Thursday", soon a second ladies' night was added. The Canterbury boomed. On May 17 1852, having

built over the bowling green, Morton opened his new hall. His opening night star act was Sam Cowell, singing 'The Ratcatcher's Daughter' and 'Villikins And His Dinah'.

At the new Canterbury, that "temple to music and the arts", women were admitted every night. There was a sixpenny refreshment ticket — which bought drinks. Three months later Morton brought in a threepenny entrance fee. But there was a problem with the division between "wet" money, and the "dry" money of the threepenny ticket. Women didn't drink, or not enough. Morton's solution was, as the evening wore on, to claim the house was full when couples arrived.

But it was a structure for respectable mass entertainment. There was a choir. Patriotic dirges such as 'Men Of Harlech' and 'Home They Brought Her Warrior Dead' were sung, while a booklet programme provided lyrics of the featured songs. Then, in December 1856, at the cost of £25,000, a new Canterbury was opened on the same site. The old hall had closed on Saturday and its replacement opened the following Monday, four days before Christmas. Morton even provided an art gallery. This earned the Canterbury the title the "Royal Academy over the water" from one of Charles Dickens's journalistic protégés, George Augustus Sala. Morton's gallery featured works by William Frith, painter of that mid-1850s sensation, *Derby Day*, and Daniel Maclise, the creator of *The Death Of Nelson*, and a friend of Dickens and the Shakespearian actor William Macready. One of Morton's big stars, singer Emily Soldene, wrote in her autobiography that it was at the Canterbury that Gounod's *Faust* was first heard in England.

And there was the food. "These artistic successes of Mr Morton's management did not deter him from seeing that the hungry supperer's chop was done to a turn," wrote Soldene. "And with his own hands (protected by a dainty serviette) he would break the succulent baked potato on to the customer's plate, where it fell in a snowy shower, sweet-smelling, soft, floury and hot, ye gods so hot!"

The new wave developed across London. The material might not be very different, but the pay for the stars was, and so was the size of the halls which rivalled, or exceeded theatres. Only the pleasure gardens could pull in bigger crowds, and, the Crystal Palace aside, the gardens were slowly, but inexorably being rained on, paved over, closed — after riots in

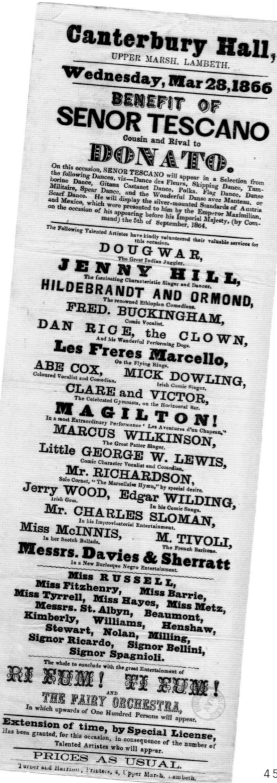

45

A ticket to the future at the Canterbury; labelled the 'Royal Academy over the water'.

JANUARY 27th

COMPLIMENTARY FREE PASS

For Exhibiting the various Bills, Programmes, &c., of the

CANTERBURY HALL,

WESTMINSTER BRIDGE ROAD,

Licensed to Mr. F. VILLIERS,

UNDER THE MANAGEMENT of Mr. W. JOHNSON,

(Late of the South London Palace.)

Admit a Gentleman & Friend

TO THE HALL,

Doors open at 7.0.   Commence at 7.30.

No person under the age of 21 admitted with this order, and must be suitably attired.   Children in Arms not admitted.

Any person selling this Order will be prosecuted for Felony.

the case of Highbury Barn — and driven out of business.

In 1856 the rebuilt Evans Music hall opened in Covent Garden. In Wapping John Wilton began turning the Mahogany Bar into Wilton's Music Hall, a task he completed in 1859. In 1857 Weston's music hall, which forty years later was to become the Frank Matcham-designed Holborn Empire, opened. In 1860 came the 1500-seater Islington Empire.

On March 26 1861 Morton moved into

London's West End. On the corner of Tottenham Court Road and Oxford Street there had been a rundown coaching inn, the Boar and Castle. On that site Morton built, at a cost of £35,000, the 1800-seat Oxford Music Hall. It was proclaimed as "not only the place for music and amusement; but a place to lunch, dine and sup at till one o'clock in the morning." It opened, with an eye on the new mainstream market, with a concert by two opera stars.

Soldene was impressed. The Italian-style hall was decorated with frescoes, gildings lights, she recalled, the side-bars covered with flowers, coloured glass, glittering, brass-bound barrels, and bottles. But "the brightest, most glittering, and most attractive thing about the bars (of course, not counting the drinks) were the barmaids."

So respectable or not, Morton had not neglected sex. "Chappies" and "Johnnies" — young men on the town — were key customers. So were "daughters of joy". "Most good people think that excess of fortune and lots of drink may induce ossification of the heart and memory in these poor girls," wrote Soldene. "They are wrong and many a night have I, 'by request' sung 'Home Sweet Home' because 'I made 'em cry'."

So taken was Morton with his success at the Oxford, that he sold the Canterbury. Then, on February 10 1868, Emily Soldene closed that night's show at the Oxford with 'Launch The Lifeboat'. A couple of hours later, Morton, passing by, saw an ominous, flickering light

Charles Morton: One of the first into the halls, he worked on into the twentieth century.

inside the hall. It was the occupational hazard of Victorian entertainment. That night the hall burned down. Morton would manage more music halls and theatres, tour the United States with Soldene, and only retire in 1904, but when that first Oxford was destroyed, Morton's pivotal role in the halls would pass with it.

Gypsying, a long time ago

Memories of mighty artistes.... memories of the Grand Opera, memories that, impalpable and gauze-like, elude one and get mixed up with the gay and festive Music Hall. Ah! The days when we went gypsying, a long time ago.

<small>THE SINGER EMILY SOLDENE LOOKING BACK, FROM AUSTRALIA IN 1897, ON HER CAREER.</small>

EMILY SOLDENE PASSED her 1865 audition with Charles Morton at the Canterbury Music Hall. Indeed at the Canterbury, said Emily, she worked alongside the young Emma Crouch, who went on to become *la grande horizontale*, Cora Pearl, in Paris.

Emily who also performed in her early days as Miss Fitzhenry — which is how she debuted in 1864 at London's St James' Hall — went on to sing Verdi, Bellini, Donnizetti, Offenbach and 'Up The Alma Heights' (clambering to a top A) at the Oxford Music Hall. And, after the destruction of that first Oxford, Soldene continued to work frequently with Morton. It was with him, at the Islington Philharmonic theatre in 1871, that she had her first major hit in Offenbach's *Geneviève de Brabant*. "In a very short time the dirty old 'Phil' evolved into a bright gay little theatre," she recalled, "with quite an important stage, private boxes, blue stain curtains, and a magnificent bar, extending the whole length of the corridor, with magnificent barmaids doing magnificent business."

Confirmed as a light opera star, in a company with Morton, she toured Australasia and North America. "The first thing I had to eat in New York was at Delmonico's in 14th Street, oysters and champagne," she wrote. "Fourteenth Street was smart then, and no stores disturbed its aristocratic calm. We put up at the Fifth Avenue Hotel, which was rather expensive and our first bill $255 for five days

and three persons."

Back in Britain she took the first English-language *Carmen* on tour outside London, and, back in the United States played Broadway, and settled in San Francisco in the early 1890s.

Emily got around. She had received two offers of marriage while travelling on the American railroad, "the would-be bridegroom, in one case offering to a find a parson on board the train and have the thing settled 'right away'. I have been as near as possible 'side-tracked' by the handsomest cowboy in Arizona, Colonel Charles Spencer. I have been 'snowed in' at Truckee, and 'washed out' on the Plains. I have lunched on the summit of the Rockies, and mailed a post-card (which was safely delivered) to London from the summit of the Sierras. I have been down a silver mine in Virginia City, where the temperature was so high you had to take a hot bath before returning to the surface, and I have been up a mountain in the same locality an hour later, gathering ice to eat with the strawberries just arrived from 'Frisco. I have eaten bear's pad in St Louis, and been introduced to native and growling lions at Green River."

She lost money on another Australian tour — "I say that on the vast continent of Australia no such thing as a music hall exists" — switched careers and became a writer and gossip columnist for the *Sydney Evening News* and other papers.

Emily's was a career that took in singing,

The great Emily Soldene, an early arrival in the mixed media world...

touring, producing and writing around the world until her death in Bloomsbury in 1912. She was a sometime sex symbol, an earner — and loser — of big money, and, by the 1880s, part of a new mass media world, where divisions between low-brow and middle-brow were breaking down, where the old "pot-house" music halls were vanishing. A tide of art for the common people was sweeping the world. Emily rode the wave.

The greasy sidewalk

Going to the Canterbury was dreadful. I remember the shock I got when I went under the railway arch, down the dingy, dirty narrow street, the greasy sidewalk, the muddy gutter, full of dirty babies, the commonplace-looking public house. I felt I could not go in, but I did. The people were polite and showed me upstairs; there was lots of sawdust. Soon I found myself in a long picture gallery, at the other end of which a rehearsal was being held. The pictures delighted but the smell of beer and stale tobacco smoke revolted me. I have since been told that one that day I held my head very high and by my manner conveyed my utmost scorn for the Canterbury and all its surroundings.

EMILY SOLDENE RECALLING HER AUDITION AT CHARLES MORTON'S CANTERBURY MUSIC HALL IN 1865.

I WENT LOOKING for Charles Morton. The places of his adolescence — the Garrick and the Pavilion — are dust. The latter survived long enough to be bombed during the Second World War Blitz on Whitechapel and was finally demolished in the early 1960s, just as the old Jewish East End began fading into history. The Oxford, Morton's Oxford, had vanished on that night nearly one and a half centuries ago. It was rebuilt, of course, went through several incarnations, but is gone now — to be replaced by a more packaged form of entertainment, the Oxford Street Virgin Megastore.

But just as great monasteries vanish and little churches survive, so there is still a St George's Tavern, on Belgrave Road in Pimlico, where Morton began his free-and-easies in the 1840s, a fine Victorian building. No glees or singing now, and what remains of its "sporting" reputation on the night I got there amounted to televised football and studying racing form.

And then there was the Canterbury. That too had been repeatedly rebuilt. Lambeth Council's archives left an intriguing phone message. Yes, said a cheery female London voice, there is an Upper Marsh, and there was a Canterbury, but then so much has changed off Westminster Bridge Road, there was the Blitz, and there was all that redevelopment... The bombs hit it in 1942. The redevelopment came in the 1950s.

It was a bitter night; I wandered the Waterloo Road, made my way past County Hall and the Saatchi art gallery and the Aquarium and along the river and arrived amidst the traffic swarming across the Thames, at a roundabout sling-shotting traffic out on the Dover Road. And then there was that vast silver 1990s structure of the Paris–London Eurotunnel rail terminal. But beyond that was The Cut. I crossed the dog-end of Westminster Bridge Road and stumbled into nineteenth-century darkness. There was Emily Soldene's railway arch, and beyond that, a dingy, dirty narrow street, a greasy sidewalk and a muddy gutter. In the noise and the rain I wished for, anticipated even, Morton and Sam Cowell and Emily Soldene and, who knows, Cora Pearl, back on a day trip from Paris. Not there of course; instead desolate Upper Marsh revealed postwar council housing, with St Thomas's Hospital as the backdrop. No dirty babies, not even the commonplace-looking public house. It is difficult to place it precisely, Lambeth had said, but Canterbury House is very close.

Canterbury House, a darkened 1960s scaffolded block, is the heir and space of the Royal Academy Over The Water, that London cradle for Gounod's *Faust*. The physical traces of that past are quite lost, which is why perhaps, in those lone and level marshes, they survive so well in the mind.

Now there is a high-rise: The Canterbury near Waterloo.

A riot in Astor Place

*"I'm bilein' over for a sousin' good fight with someone somewhere.
If I don't have a muss soon, I'll spile."*
MOSE, THE "BOWERY B'HOY" HERO OF BENJAMIN A. BAKER'S SMASH-HIT OF
THE LATE 1840S, *NEW YORK AS IT IS.*

FROM THE BEGINNING the Englishman
William Macready and the American Edwin
Forrest were performers of contrasting styles,
and contrasting backgrounds. Yet stage rivalry
doesn't usually explode into violence and death.
But then the careers of actors and show business
don't usually collide quite so spectacularly with
big money, cheap journalism, xenophobia,
property speculation, class war, pulp fiction —
and the birth of American stardom.

New York's Astor Place Riot of 1849 features
bloody tragedy and low farce, and ideas about
snooty English, no-nonsense Americans — and
Italian opera. The riot embraced an empire
beginning to peak, and one impatient to be
born, the low-brow and the high-brow, and
provided pointers on how show business was to
develop, even into the twenty-first century.
Events at the Astor Place Opera House also laid
down some ground rules about keeping
audiences happy and making them mad.

Macready was the grandson of an
upholsterer. He was born in 1793, just off the
Euston Road in London and educated at
Rugby School until, when he was fifteen, his
family's fortunes took a turn for the worse. He
had to leave school, and was thus denied the
chance to make a career as a lawyer, or in the
Church. Instead, slightly grudgingly, he
followed his father into acting and tried to turn
that trade into a profession instead.

He was, said the critic and writer Leigh
Hunt, one of the "plainest and most awkwardly

made men who ever trod the stage. His voice is
even coarser than his personage."

But Macready was a fine actor, albeit, at first,
usually cast as a villain. He lacked the charisma
of his great English contemporary Edmund
Kean, who, on stage, embodied passion,
conviction, and power, the very stuff indeed of
that early nineteenth-century era of
romanticism. But then Macready also lacked
Kean's alcoholism. That saw the great tragedian
plunge into an abyss, and death in 1833.

By then Macready was an established star, the
man who was considered to have snatched the
Covent Garden Theatre from financial ruin in
1819 with his performance as Richard III. And
in 1826 Macready made a well-received debut
in New York, at the Park Theatre. While in the
city he saw a 24-year-old, Edwin Forrest,
playing Julius Caesar at the Bowery Theatre.

Forrest was neither plain nor awkward, and
had not begun his career playing villains. Born
in 1802 in Philadelphia, he had used acrobatics
to build his frail physique into an intensely
muscular five foot ten. He first appeared on
stage in his late teens and in 1821 saw the man
who, he claimed, became his inspiration,
Edmund Kean, playing at the Walnut Theatre in
his hometown. After work with a touring
company on the American frontier Forrest
spent a colourful two years in New Orleans,
including a spell with an Indian chief, before
returning to the east coast.

In the mid-1830s Forrest arrived in Europe,

and was acclaimed for his performance as Spartacus at Drury Lane. But not everyone had been impressed. The Englishwoman Fanny Trollope, writing in the early 1830s, had already seen Forrest perform: "What he may become I will not pretend to prophesy;" she wrote "but when I saw him play Hamlet at Cincinnati, not even Mrs Drake's sweet Ophelia could keep me beyond the third act." It was a foretaste of things to come.

In 1837 Forrest became betrothed to an English woman, Catherine Sinclair. The marriage ceremony took place at the "actor's church", St Paul's in Covent Garden (where the fictional Eliza Doolittle would ply her flower-selling trade at the century's end) and those in attendance included William Macready. Six years later, when the Englishman made his second American tour, Forrest was amongst those who paid their respects.

By 1845, when the American returned to London, the relationship between the two men had soured. Forrest had long established himself as a prototype of that contradictory romantic American hero, extraordinary and ordinary, the guy who stands up tall for democracy, a John Wayne for the mid-nineteenth century — with a touch, perhaps, of Sylvester Stallone thrown in. Forrest was an idol to the New York's white working class, indigenous and immigrant alike, a model of the self-made man symbolised in the 1830s by Democrat President Andrew Jackson. This United States was to be a dynamic, no-nonsense country, building itself up to take over a continent, and tough guys like Forrest were the people to do it. Boats were named after him, so were racehorses and militias and volunteer fire brigades. Yet despite such a following — or fan base — Forrest declined invitations from friends like New York politician Isaiah Rynders to run for political office.

But Forrest's act was no longer surviving the Atlantic crossing. Fanny Trollope had said she "cannot admire this celebrated performer" and she, in the London of 1845, was joined by others. His Macbeth was mauled by critics and the public. The American actor accused Macready of orchestrating that hostility, and he journeyed to Edinburgh to hiss the Englishman's Hamlet. The rivalry between the two performers became big news.

The late 1840s were a time of turmoil. Across continental Europe 1848 was the year of revolutions — and repression. In Britain the popular democracy of the Chartist movement was locked in a conflict with the old landed aristocracy and the new industrialists. The peasant society of British-ruled Ireland was being devastated by the potato blight and ensuing famine. Irish nationalism was a potent force before the famine; it was incandescent after it, and nowhere more so than in the great cities of the American east coast.

Immigrants from Britain, Ireland and continental Europe flooded into New York. In 1830 the city's population was just over

> *Farewell, Macready, since this night we part,*
> *Go, take thine honour home...*
> *Thine is it that our drama did not die,*
> *Nor flicker down to brainless pantomime,*
> *And those gilt-gauds men-children swarm to see.*
> ALFRED, LORD TENNYSON'S *ODE TO W.C. MACREADY* (1851).

200,000. By 1840 Manhattan had extended as far as 20th Street, and the population had topped 312,000. By 1850 there were more than half a million inhabitants, and the slum horror of places like Five Points, Shanty-Town, Den Of Thieves and Murderers Alley symbolised a kind of city that the rich despised, and feared.

The result was a mixture waiting to explode. Within it was what was seen as an effete, Anglophile elite; and the old, and new immigrant, working classes. The detonation occurred in 1849 at Astor Place on Broadway, where the 18-month-old Astor Opera House had gone up for the "eliteet" enjoyment of

Italian opera and upmarket acting, by the properly dressed, shaved, and groomed Anglophile element of New York society.

Astor Place was off Lafayette Place, which at that time was home to John Jacob Astor, the banker E.D. Morgan, Warren Delano, grandfather of Franklin Delano Roosevelt, and a coterie of other bankers, dealers and merchants. And if anything symbolised that coterie, it was the neo-classical Opera House. There were (at first) no press tickets for journalists, there were no decent cheap seats, but there was plenty of foreign non-American opera, and on May 7 1849, came the night that the hapless 56-year-

A New York opening that encountered hostile reviews... The bloody Astor Place riot that accompanied Englishman William Macready's interpretation of Macbeth in 1849.

The evening of May 7 had been orchestrated, partly, by Forrest's friend Isaiah Rynders. Macready was greeted on stage with cries of "Down with the codfish aristocracy!" accompanied by the hurling of rotten fruit and vegetables, eggs, a bottle of stinking asafoetida, and coins. As the performance progressed, or degenerated, the missiles included chairs, thrown from the balcony. With the third act the Englishman retired from the stage. He promptly announced he was heading back to England.

His intention was greeted with dismay by the circle around Lafayette Place. If Macready quit, what would it mean in the greater scheme of power? Across Europe a few months before it had meant narrowly averted revolution. No performance by Macready in Macbeth meant caving in to the world of the Bowery — to colourfully suited, red-flannel-shirted, slick-haired rude b'hoys sousing for a fight.

Two days later Macready was backed by a range of wealthy supporters, and by writers Washington Irving and Herman Melville, in a notice in the *New York Herald*. Across the political divide adventurer and pioneer pulp fiction writer Ned Buntline had become head of an "American Committee". Its handbill "Shall Americans Or English Rule In This City?" — penned by Rynders — was plastered across New York and urged workers to "express their opinions at the English aristocratic opera house". Meanwhile, at City Hall, a new mayor, Caleb Woodhull, took office.

By May 10 Macready had accepted an invitation to return to the Scottish play, with a guarantee that subsequent performances would be

old London tragedian, William Charles Macready, tried to play Macbeth.

For the elite Forrest was, by then, out of fashion. But this didn't matter below Canal Street, at the Broadway Theatre — which was traditionally adorned with a vast Stars and Stripes — where Forrest was also appearing in Macbeth. Macready had been on tour in the US for some time, dogged by Forrest, to a largely appreciative reception, although there had been the odd incident — half a sheep's carcase was hurled on stage in Cincinnati, but that was the normal small change of show business. Things would be different at Astor Place.

A very special relationship: William Macready (*left*) Edwin Forrest (*right*).

properly policed. Thus reassured, that night, at 7.30, he stepped back on to the Opera House stage.

Macready's confidence was misplaced. New York's police chief had told Woodhull that he lacked the resources to handle a major disturbance. The new mayor responded by having three hundred and fifty soldiers stationed at nearby Washington Square. Rynders and Buntline had their ten thousand march up from Dover Street, and from around the city. At quarter past nine, as the crowd battered on the Opera House doors, the military arrived, and soon after opened fire, first into the air, then into the ranks of enraged New Yorkers. It was the first time that the militia had been used against a mob in New York since the Revolutionary War. By the end of it there were twenty-two dead or dying. Most of them were workers, most of them were native-born, but seven of them were Irishmen. There were one hundred and fifty injured and one hundred and seventeen arrests; among them was Buntline, who was sentenced to a year in prison.

The Opera House never recovered, and soon closed. And there would be no more public displays of exclusivity around such ventures. Yet the divisions between "high art" and "low entertainment" would persist whether the city was London, New York, Montreal or Paris.

And the actors? Forrest's marriage ended in disarray after he physically attacked a journalist who had been backing his wife in a marital dispute. There was a flurry of law suits, all of which he lost, and all of which attracted vast attention from the press. In between seclusion in his Philadelphia home, Forrest made several comebacks. In 1872, after a performance in San Francisco, he died, but not before playing a key role in establishing, on the American stage, the idea of the star, the focus of a public adulation never achieved by his own supposed hero, Edmund Kean.

As for Macready, he headed back to London via Boston, made a farewell tour in 1851, retired to Cheltenham — where he died in 1873 — and had a son, who was to become the commander of British forces in Ireland during the Irish War of Independence in 1921.

Potato nose

The catalyst was Phineas T. Barnum, as it so often was in the early days of the entertainment trade. The result was the first exercise in the production and control of transatlantic show business. In 1850 the promoter and showman paid thirty-year-old Jenny Lind $150,000 to give 150 performances in the United States and Cuba.

Lind was not beautiful — she had, she said, a "potato nose" — but she had a stunning soprano voice, and had taken Berlin and London by storm. Queen Victoria had thrown her own bouquet to Lind at her 1848 London debut, and the Duke of Wellington attended that entire run. A range of souvenirs, scents, handkerchiefs, books and other keepsakes were marketed. After two more London seasons came the trip to the United States.

In New York Barnum backed up his investment with a huge marketing campaign which — to attract women — emphasised virtue, as well as the talent of "the Swedish Nightingale".

It worked. Thirty thousand New Yorkers came out for her arrival. The deeply religious Lind made a fortune, and so did Barnum — although she broke with him two-thirds of the way through her tour.

In 1852 Jenny married Otto Goldschmidt, a young German-Jewish banker in Boston. Back in Europe, she retired from singing, and in 1858, settled in England. The woman who was perhaps the first great transatlantic star, became herself a daughter of the Empire, appointed by the Prince of Wales, four years before her death in 1887, professor of singing at the new Royal College of Music.

First star of the north: Jenny Lind.

Legs like pump handles

…In the full foam of wrath and dread
To me the desert-born was led:
They bound me on, that menial throng,
Upon his back with many a thong;
They loosed him with a sudden lash —
Away! — away! and on we dash!
FROM LORD BYRON'S *MAZEPPA* (1818).

IN 1861, AT the Green Street Theatre in Albany, New York, the dancer, actress, poet, adventurer and woman of mystery Adah Isaacs Menken climbed on a horse and dashed headlong into history. For in a stage adaptation of Byron's epic, Adah played Mazeppa, the hero of the tale. For the part Adah appeared on stage in a doublet and tights, giving an impression — to the more susceptible elements of mid-Victorian society — of near-nudity.

Adah, who was probably born Ada McCord in Memphis Tennessee, or may have been born in New Orleans, or Madrid, depending on the accounts she gave, had previously enjoyed modest theatrical success, but from that night on, everything changed. "The Menken", as she was known, was introducing the "leg show" to the North American and European stage. After Albany she took Mazeppa to Nevada and California — she was a big success in Bohemian San Francisco — and by 1864 the show was at Astley's Theatre on the south side of Westminster Bridge in London. Her show was not well-received by *Punch* magazine:

…Here's half the town — if bills be true —
To Astley's nightly thronging,
To see "the Menken" throw aside
All to her sex belonging.
Stripping off women's modesty

With women's outward trappings —
A bare-backed jade on
bare-backed steed…

Others were more enthusiastic, including sell-out audiences, Charles Dickens, and Dante Gabriel Rosetti. She was even more wildly acclaimed in Paris, and befriended by George Sand, amongst others. Later she played Vienna, and London, again.

By then legs were becoming a feature of other stage performances. The cancan, that dance born in the cultural collision between France and Algeria, had been popular in Paris in the 1830s. Assisted by the composer Offenbach in the 1850s, it began to spread. Enter the Hungarian dancer, Imre Kiralfy, his brother and their sisters, who, claimed Emily Soldene, met Charles Morton in the 1860s — around the time that *Punch* was denouncing Adah — and introduced the cancan to the Oxford music hall. Haniola Kiralfy was a sensation, holding on to a post, while her brothers worked her legs "like pump handles… prior to her executing the most extraordinary gyrations and the highest kicking that had previously been seen on any stage".

Imre, who lived on until 1919, went on to stage a series of vast dance spectacles in the United States, often working with Phineas Barnum. His career climaxed with his construction of the "Great White City" in west London — the name survives — which coincided with the 1908 Olympic games.

But Haniola was dead by 1889. Adah Isaacs Menken, meanwhile, ravaged by a mysterious illness, had died in 1868, aged thirty-three, in Paris. And her own notoriety was overshadowed when, that same year, the actress and dancer Lydia Thompson, plus her British Blondes, promoted by Phineas Barnum, leapt to fame at Wood's Museum And Menagerie on New York's 30th Street.

Two years earlier, at Niblo's Garden, a 500-performance run of *The Black Crook* had begun. The audience for this proto-American musical had arrived primarily because of the gratuitous (in plot terms) appearance of a lightly clad female dance troupe. The market was there, and what Lydia and her company then did from 1868 until her last visit to the United States in 1891 was to provide a basis for burlesque and vaudeville dancing in Empires, Alhambras and Roxys for a century. Just then it triggered another round of moral outrage.

Lydia, a Londoner, was in her early thirties when she and the other three blondes arrived in the United States. Hers was the first organised British company to make such a trip — the second would be that of Charles Morton and Emily Soldene.

After debuting in London in 1852, Thompson had become hugely successful, touring Europe, and the Russian Empire. A handout (her own) claimed that in Helsinki "her pathway was strewn with flowers and the streets illuminated with torches carried by her ardent admirers. At Cologne, the students insisted on sending the horses about their business, and drawing the carriage that contained the object of their devotion themselves. At Riga and other Russian towns on the Baltic, it became

Dress codes have changed: Lydia Thompson, 'the British Blonde', recreating a very special Robinson Crusoe, with parrot.

59

an almost universal custom to exhibit her portrait on one side of the stove to correspond with that of the Czar on the other side. At Lember, a captain Ludoc Baumbarten of the Russian Dragoons took some flowers and a glove belonging to Miss Thompson, placed them on his breast; then shot himself through the heart, leaving on his table a note stating that his love for her brought on the fatal act."

From 1868 to 1874 Thompson and her troupe were out of Britain, touring the United States from coast to coast — she and another dancer horsewhipped the editor of the *Chicago Times* following a bad review — and they went on to Australia and India. This was mass culture, on tour thanks to steamships and railways, reaching out across the English-speaking world, and into the world of the Empire. Her last performance, four years before her death in 1908, was as the Duchess of Albuquerque in *A Queen's Romance*, at the Imperial Theatre in London.

They don't care a curse for what others might say

You may talk about your Broadway belles, your Fifth Avenue swells, your exquisitely dressed creatures, with their lavender kids and their la de das, now what do they know about enjoyment? They are afraid to go in for a little fun for disarranging their toilets: and then what would Mrs Grundy say? "Charles Frederick Augustus is getting decidedly vulgar; Serephina Emelia is positively shocking!" But here in the Bowery people enjoy themselves just when they feel like it. They don't care a curse for what others might say, for that's the custom.
TONY PASTOR IN 1874.

AT THE AGE of eleven, in 1843, New Yorker Antonio Pastori, the son of a Greenwich Village violinist-cum-barber-cum-fruit shop proprietor was singing at temperance meetings. Two years later he was performing at Phineas Taylor Barnum's American Museum in New York. Barnum, the definitive showman, boasted of "living statuary, tableaux, Gipsies, Albinos, fat boys" at the Museum. He billed the thirteen-year-old, then developing a line in blackface minstrelsy, as an "infant prodigy".

Tony Pastor kept singing, began clowning and, despite parental disapproval, embarked on a circus career. By the mid-1850s he was established as a comic singer, and had begun to write his own, topical songs. On the eve of the Civil War he was back in New York, performing at the New York American Concert Hall, a saloon at 444 Broadway. Thirty years later he recalled that, at "444" observing how the place worked, he "determined that if women could also be induced to attend, the patronage could be materially extended".

Phineas T Barnum had already cleaned up his American Museum. And Pastor's was that same revelation that was then transforming British popular entertainment. And it came little more than a decade after the Astor Place riot, which, having pitched Bowery B'hoys against New York's elite, had demarcated popular entertainment in the city. Pastor realised that the material coming out of the

Bowery, while attracting those seen as "rowdy girls", was not for "respectable" women or families. With the War Pastor, pursuing a boisterous pro-Union populist line effectively emerged as the city's — indeed the country's — first vaudeville star, even if "vaudeville" was a term he professed to despise for its foreignness.

In 1865 Pastor's Opera House opened at 201 Bowery. Its star was Pastor, and as its proprietor he made his pitch for family business. Alcohol sales were regulated, obscene acts curbed, "ladies invitation nights" offered free admission for accompanied women, while prize giveaways delivered hams and turkeys, flour and coal. That new audience had emerged.

As the city's focus continued to move up town, Pastor followed, opening a larger theatre in 1875 at 585-587 Broadway, with matinees for women and children. Six years later his last word in entertainment, the 1000-seat New Fourteenth Street Theatre in the Tammany Building on Third Avenue at Union Square opened. The family audience had arrived, smoking and alcohol were confined to a saloon; the New Fourteenth symbolised the variety that had transformed the Bowery tradition while remaining within it. Pastor meanwhile continued to feature on three-hour bills which provided launch pads for many vaudeville stars. Introducing acts, singing topical "rhymes for the times", he linked that riotous mid-nineteenth century Bowery

with the vaudeville which dominated American entertainment into the 1920s — and anticipated a world which would keep the David Letterman television show located on Broadway in the twenty-first century.

Uptown from Downtown: Tony Pastor took show business out of the Bowery and into the family.

TONY PASTOR.

61

Blackface

The filthy scum of white society, who have stolen from us a complexion denied to them by nature, in which to make money and pander to the corrupt taste of their white fellow citizens.

THE AFRICAN-AMERICAN JOURNALIST AND CIVIL RIGHTS CAMPAIGNER FREDERICK DOUGLASS, IN 1848, WRITING ABOUT WHITE MINSTREL TROUPES.

BEFORE THE RISE of vaudeville late in the nineteenth century, minstrelsy — where, originally, white performers "blacked up" in caricature of African-Americans — was a dominant form in popular American entertainment. It was at a time when slavery, before and after its abolition in 1865, was part of popular consciousness, myth, fantasy, guilt and nightmare. While racist to its core, early minstrelsy did have within it an exciting echo of black America. Minstrelsy could provide sentimentality — and it could provide an escape. It was a place where whites, in cities where everything that was solid promptly melted into air, could see other ethnic groups, the aspiring, the bums and the swells lampooned, and bewildering change alchemised into show business.

"Ethiopean delineators" like Thomas D. Rice, phenomenally successful with his Jim Crow routine in New York and London in the 1830s, were followed by the appearance, at the Bowery Amphitheatre in Manhattan in 1843, of the four-strong Virginia Minstrels. Within months the Virginia Minstrels had taken London by storm.

The roots of minstrelsy were in the industrial cities of the north-eastern US — Boston, Philadelphia and, particularly, New York. The success of the Virginia Minstrels inspired a host of rival acts. By the 1850s the shows had become bigger and more ambitious. They mixed song and dance, humour and sketches — and claimed, among other things, to be authentic reproductions of the joys of southern slave folk culture.

After the American Civil War, minstrelsy changed. African-Americans, seeking a way into show business, became "colored" — rather than the whites' "nigger" — minstrels themselves. Compelled to follow white stereotypes about blacks, they also usually ended up with white managers. The first black minstrels had appeared in the mid-1850s, post-1865 the companies, emphasising their "plantation" authenticity, helped refocus the white

The great Eddie Cantor (born Isidore Itszkowitz) debuted at Clinton's Music Hall in New York in the Teddy Roosevelt era, was a Broadway star in the 1920s, a Hollywood and radio star from the 1930s and into television by 1950. Cantor stuck his neck out, whether the cause was Union rights, opposition to far-right politicians, the fight against polio — or saving Jewish kids from the Nazis. Yet he too was once part of the blackface generation...

From here to eternity: The first and last Queen-Empress with the man who made some of it possible, Benjamin Disraeli, the first and last Earl of Beaconsfield.

vast empires, lose out to empresses.

The problem was exacerbated in 1874. Victoria's second son, Prince Alfred, Duke of Edinburgh, married Tsar Alexander II's daughter Grand Duchess Marie Alexandrovna in St Petersburg. Relations with the Russian Empire were already strained and once again the relative status of empires and kingdoms intruded.

Disraeli was adept at handling the Queen. By January 1876, the prime minister was moving towards providing Victoria with the new title. "What might have been looked upon as an ebullition of individual vanity," he confided to Lord Salisbury, "may bear the semblance of deep and organised policy." That May the legislation went through Parliament. In August Benjamin Disraeli became the Earl of Beaconsfield. On January 1, 1877, Victoria signed herself Victoria R&I (Victoria, Regina et Imperatrix — Queen and Empress) for the first time. There had been a first, informal British Empire based on North America in the 18th century. That had been lost. A new informal empire had grown up in the wake of British conquest in the nineteenth century. Now the show had a formal title.

Victoria, the four-foot-ten Queen-Empress, a tad taller than Little Tich, the music hall act, only just emerging out of a decade of seclusion, was being placed in the spotlight as the icon of the age of empires. It was a process boosted by parades, pageantry, imperial awards and titles, electric telegraphs, cheap prints, popular newspapers and by the new music halls, Gaieties, Hippodromes, Pavilions, Victorias — and, most of all, Empires.

By jingo if we do

The Dogs of War are loose and the rugged Russian Bear,
All bent on blood and robbery has crawled out of his lair...
It seems a thrashing now and then will never help to tame...
That brute, and so he's out upon the same old game.
The Lion did his best... to find him some excuse...
To crawl back to his den again. All efforts were no use...
He hunger'd for his victim. He's pleased when blood is shed...
But let us hope his crimes may all recoil on his own head...
Chorus:
We don't want to fight but by jingo if we do...
We've got the ships, we've got the men, and got the money too!
We've fought the Bear before... and while we're Britons true,
The Russians shall not have Constantinople...

From 'Macdermott's Warsong', the 'Jingo Song' composed by George W. Hunt, first performed by Gilbert Hastings Macdermott, May 1877.

THE SCANNING MAY be bad, but the timing was perfect. The chorus still resonates in the twenty-first century, and the impact of the 'Jingo Song' helped lock British music hall into a new, commercialised patriotism, and a new, packaged empire. Queen Victoria had been Empress of India for five months, and, under Benjamin Disraeli (the Earl of Beaconsfield), Britain was teetering on the edge of war with Imperial Russia. Indeed early in 1878 a Royal Navy squadron was to be sent through the Dardanelles in a show of strength.

At that time Macdermott had been working in Britain and the United States as an actor, playwright — he wrote and featured in an adaptation of Charles Dickens's *The Mystery of Edwin Drood* — and singer. Hunt's songwriting meanwhile had taken in comic work, and edged into politics with a song supporting the American anti-slavery movement.

The success of the 'Jingo Song' was a phenomenon. It created a new word, Jingoism, for extreme, mindless patriotism. It made Macdermott, the *Great* Macdermott, a huge star. The singer also came out with follow-ups. There was 'True Blue For Ever' in 1879, and, after Disraeli's death in 1881, 'The Flower Our Hero Loved'. Disraeli surely deserved it; he was the man who had launched the empire as a brand, and inaugurated in Britain a new era of saleable right-wingery whose sentiments echoed around the music halls.

As for the singer, the sport that Macdermott loved was horseracing. In 1885 he was declared bankrupt. He quit the stage in 1894, and died in May 1901, a little more than three months after the passing of the first, and last, supreme Queen-Empress.

An ensemble of amusements

Upwards of four hundred people of all ages, men and women, were employed in this grand spectacle, which was rendered doubly interesting, by the introduction of real Cossack horses, mounted by that singular militia; by the costumes of all the different nations placed under the sway of Russia; and by those of the warriors belonging to each nation. The profusion of gold and glittering ornaments, particularly in the head-dress of the Russian and Tartar women; the variety and singularity of the costumes, many of which were exceedingly pretty; the succession of so many national dances, of most of which I had never formed the least idea, and in one or two of which shone conspicuous the pretty and active mimic dancer... presented even to my own passive and stoical imagination an ensemble of amusements worthy of the capital.

THE BRITISH ROYAL PHYSICIAN A.B. GRANVILLE, REVIEWING THE "PANTOMIME BALLET" ON A VISIT TO THE ST. PETERSBURG IMPERIAL THEATRE IN 1827.

TSARIST SPECTACLE ASIDE, A.B. Granville had mixed feelings about nights out at the Imperial. Its interior was a "sorry copy" of a Parisian playhouse. It was smaller than Covent Garden, but well-heated and the orchestra was "really very good". But the opera was "neither of the best or most pleasing kind" and as for the farce, the "distinct and prosy manner of delivery of the ladies in particular gave the thing the appearance of a girls' school".

Granville would have had to wait another half century before the Tsar's capital got itself a more splendid Imperial. In 1878 the Imperial Theatre on the Fontanka opened. This was not, like later British Empire theatres, an improvisation on a theme of Empire, a shrewd exploitation of a name, but Imperial, part of the edifice of the autocracy. The stunning theatre, designed by L.F. Fontana, was completed in 1878. Three years later the first Tsar to enter it, Alexander II, the man who freed Russia's serfs, was blown up by a bomb thrown by a member of the People's Will group.

The theatre lived on. Sarah Bernhardt performed there, and Isadora Duncan danced there; meanwhile St. Petersburg became Petrograd, and Petrograd Leningrad, and Leningrad — St. Petersburg. Wars, revolution, terror, and the Nazi siege of Leningrad, which killed more than a million people, came and went, as did the Romanovs, Stalin, Krushchev, Brezhnev, Gorbachev, and Putin.

Through it all the Imperial on the Fontanka has survived. And there is an Imperial-Theater Imperium on Hamburg's Reeperbahn, a location for *Grease*, the *Rocky Horror Show* and Germany's continuing, inexplicable love affair with that Edwardian pioneer of pulp fiction, Edgar Wallace.

More upmarket is the Théâtre Impériale de Compiègne in Picardy, which has also lived through a surfeit of world history. In the mid-1860s, France's Emperor Napoleon III decided to build a theatre in Compiègne, the town to which his court moved during the hunting season. Auguste-Gabriel Ancelet was commissioned to design it and Elié Delaunay to decorate the dome of the auditorium.

Changing empires:
Russian Imperial
Ballet Company
star Lydia Kyasht
playing the Empire
in London in 1913.

LYDIA KYASHT
AT THE
EMPIRE
A Study by Bassano

Changing empires: Russian Imperial Ballet Company star Lydia Kyasht playing the Empire in London in 1913.

Alas, for Imperial dreams; in 1870 came the Franco-Prussian war, Compiègne became the headquarters of the victorious German army, the theatre was incomplete, and the Emperor and his wife departed for England. Later the theatre was completed, but war would not go away. In 1918, Compiègne was where the German armistice was signed, in a railway carriage. In that same carriage, twenty-two years later, the French surrendered to Germany. By the 1990s a group had formed to restore the 900-seat Théâtre Impériale. It was after all, as Carlo-Maria Giulini observed, one of the most acoustically perfect in the world.

Every kind of abomination

… Leicester Square such as I first remember it — a howling wilderness, with broken railings, a receptacle for dead cats and every kind of abomination; then covered over by the hideous building for Mr Wyld's great Globe…

LONDON'S PRIME ENTERTAINMENT PLAZA IN THE 1850S, RECALLED, THREE DECADES ON, BY EDMUND YATES.

LEICESTER SQUARE IN the 1960s had none of the mock-Edwardian street furniture which arrived in the 1990s, and only mild abominations, but the swirling crowds of alcohol-fuelled young out-of-towners were already a presence. That was the night I went to the next-to-last cinema incarnation of the Empire Leicester Square — words that hang together — to see David Lean's *Doctor Zhivago*. The last time I was in the Square, four decades on, kids were picking up crumpled billboards of the new Nicole Kidman movie.

No dead cats? The old Empire Leicester Square.

71

Security men were clearing away the crash barriers that had framed the spectacle, and separated the Australian star from the crowds. Leicester Square is still a place to stand and stare, and the Empire is why.

Yates's "hideous building" was the creation of the cartographer, James Wyld the younger. For a decade, from 1851, Wyld mounted a spectacular exhibition in the Square. His 60ft by 40ft gaslit globe provided vast crowds of Londoners, and visitors to the great 1851 exhibition, with something to stare at, an early insight into the wonders of a planet that the British were engaged in colonising. The globe also attracted, as Yates's observations indicated, a lot of hostile, albeit jocular criticism.

Then in the late 1850s, on the north side of the square a new, small music hall opened, and took its name from Wyld's venture. The Café du Globe was taking over a sleazy slice of London property. In the 1680s it had been Aylesbury House. As Savile House in the nineteenth century it was a sometime gambling den and song and supper room, a handicraft gallery, "Walhalla" — featuring waxworks, a clairvoyant and *poses plastiques* — and, from the late 1840s, a casino. But the Café du Globe marked a step up in the world, until the mid–1860s, when the property burned down. What followed, after a time of dereliction, was the building of the Royal London Panorama, but what it opened as, in 1884, was the Empire Theatre, which after a fleeting phase as a light opera venue emerged as the Empire Theatre of Varieties Leicester Square in 1887. It was to be a source of inspiration for music halls and theatres nationwide, and worldwide. It was also to be, almost immediately, a source of violent controversy.

John Philip Sousa, the sound of the great American republic, provided a backing track for the age of empires, and in this case the Empire Leicester Square.

More or less painted, and gorgeously dressed

Mrs. Chant stated that her attention was first called to the Empire early in the present year by two American gentlemen…They were so shocked that she determined to visit the theatre, but did not do so until July when the Living Pictures made so much stir. Early in the evening there were comparatively few people in the promenade, but after nine o'clock the number increased. She noticed young women enter alone, more or less painted, and gorgeously dressed. They accosted young gentlemen who were strangers to them, and paid little attention to the performance. She herself was so quietly attired that one of the attendants exclaimed to a woman. "You better mind how you behave tonight — there are strangers about". (Laughter)

THE DAILY TELEGRAPH, OCTOBER 11 1894 REPORTING THE TESTIMONY OF MRS LAURA ORMISTON CHANT, OPPOSING THE RENEWAL OF THE EMPIRE LEICESTER SQUARE'S ENTERTAINMENT LICENCE.

IN 1888-89 LONDONERS — or at least its male, middle class, citizens — got a say in the running of the world's biggest city. The directly-elected London County Council was created, replacing the Metropolitan Board of Works. Democracy was on the up, but this also meant that the anarchy of London music hall life was on the down.

The old halls were already under threat from the size and organisation of the wave of variety theatres when, in 1878, new fire regulations led to the closure of many small halls. Another threat came from campaigners aiming to "clean up" not just the acts, but the venues.

One target was Wilton's Music Hall in Wapping, in the East End of London. Two ladies, it was recounted in 1896, in a history of the local Wesleyan and Methodist mission, had happened to be passing Wilton's when, hearing its "dreadful hubbub" were drawn in. "The sights on stage and the entire condition of things became so awful to them, that they fell down on their knees together, in the centre of the hall, and in view of the stage and the crowd of onlookers, prayed that God would break the power of the devil in the place…"

God answered their prayers, but moved in mysterious, and ironic ways, his wonders to perform. In 1888, the year the LCC was born, the Christians took over Wilton's, that gilded palace of sin, and turned it into a mission hall. By the 1960s it had become a warehouse — which is when the LCC stepped in — to preserve it as a music hall. Thus was it still there, so that, a few years later, I could stumble on it, and, at the end of the century, watch that tale of London crime, vice and villainy, *The Beggar's Opera*, performed on its wonderful stage.

Wilton's was far from the only hall to be targeted, or indeed converted from use by the devil's hirelings, to use by the children of the almighty.

Prominent in these campaigns was the National Vigilance Association, whose leading figures included the temperance crusader Frederick Charrington, a teetotaller from a prominent brewing family.

Amongst the new LCC's tasks, via its Theatres And Music Halls Sub-Committee, was the licensing of places of public entertainment.

The LCC was then controlled by Progressives, who, not for the first or last time, were political animals who combined radicalism and puritanism.

This was the start of *Sex, Votes And Newspapers*, a British show that now plays across the western world. It boasts juicy parts for prurient players with interests in democracy, religion, entertainment, the mass media — and grandstanding. It has never closed, but famous among its opening performances was that staged at the Empire Leicester Square.

As soon as the sub-committee came into existence — and on which Charrington served — groups like the NVA were targeting music halls as centres of vice, and pressing the LCC for action. An attack in the early 1890s on the Leicester Square Empire had failed. Campaigners stumbled under cross-examination, presented their case badly — and modesty itself stopped them making clear just what they were complaining about. So their battle temporarily refocused on halls in working-class areas in the East End of London like Wiltons.

But by 1894 they had resumed their work in the West End. One target was the Palace Theatre with its *tableaux vivants*, "living pictures" in which artistic masterpieces were recreated, employing what an LCC inspector described as "apparently nude, or semi-nude women". Bids to cancel its licence failed. But then there was the Leicester Square Empire — and in that year too the pair of male American tourists, solicited by upmarket prostitutes in the music hall's promenade, reacted by complaining to Mrs Laura Ormiston Chant of the British Woman's Temperance Association. In the same way that the music hall business was a trade around the Atlantic rim, so was the trade in moral outrage.

It was a time when more and more women,

while still denied the vote, were moving into frontline politics. One of those was Ormiston Chant. Following on from the Americans came her visit to the Leicester Square Empire. She then, opposing the renewal of the venue's licence, testified to the LCC committee about what she saw on her night out at the Empire. The costumes of the dancers were minimal, she explained, while the areas of what seemed to be exposed flesh were very substantial. Indeed she had had to resort to opera glasses to check if the artistes were wearing tights at all.

But the issue for the campaigners was not just about what happened behind the footlights; it was about the combustive mix of what consequently went on in front of them. There were no barriers between the auditorium, the Empire's bars and the Empire's promenades. And it was on those promenades that some of the West End's more upmarket prostitutes solicited their clients. At the Empire the apparently complex codes of late Victorian England were easily deciphered except, it seemed, by outraged transatlantic visitors. Only a prostitute would look a man in the eye. Only a prostitute would, occasionally, make physical contact. Indecent dancing plus alcohol equalled the promotion of prostitution. It had to stop, said the campaigners, and the LCC agreed. It told the Empire that barriers had to go up between the Dress Circle and the Upper Circle and the promenades if the licence was to be renewed.

There were many reverberations from the battles of Mrs Ormiston Chant. George Bernard Shaw used her as the model for the heroine of his play *Candida*. And when canvas barriers went up at the Empire a lively mob assembled to tear them down, as the *Pall Mall Gazette* reported:

"The bar at the back had been shut off from

the promenade by means of a screen of woodwork covered with canvas... gradually the crowd began to attack the screen. Well-dressed men — some of them almost middle-aged — kicked at it from within, burst the canvas but hardly affecting the woodwork. The attendants — most of whom might have played the giant in a country show — watched in helpless and amused inactivity. Finally there was an attack on the canvas, which was torn away in strips, and passed throughout the crowd, everyone endeavouring to secure a scrap of it as a souvenir. Mr Hitchens, the manager, attempted argumentative remonstrance, but was carried away by half a dozen enthusiasts. Then the woodwork of the screen was demolished by vigorous kicks from both sides. The crowd had already cheered itself hoarse, and now began to go out into London, brandishing fragments of the screen..."

Amongst that crowd had been a twenty-year-old Sandhurst army cadet. "I now made my maiden speech," wrote Winston Churchill in *My Early Life*. "Mounting on the debris and indeed partially emerging from it, I addressed the tumultuous crowd. No very accurate report of my words has been preserved. They did not however fall unheeded and I have heard about them several times since."

It was to no avail. The barriers were reconstructed.

"Still," wrote Churchill of his venture into

OUR EMPIRE IN DANGER.
ST. GEORGE AND THE DRAGONS.

Umbrellas, moustaches and sterotypes: An 1894 cartoon shows Mrs. Ormiston Chant as the Dragon versus the male right to the pleasures of the Empire, Leicester Square.

sexual politics, "no-one can say we did not do our best".

And Churchill did not forget those days: In 1951 the war leader returned to power as prime minister. His private secretary, Sir John Colville, noted that while his memory might have lost some of its sharpness, he still quoted verses of poetry, and sung as well, "the music hall songs of the 1890s".

An Imperial dream

Weber: Who vass dat lady I seen you with last night?
Fields: She vass no lady, she vass my wife.

<small>FROM THE 1890s "MIKE AND MEYER" ROUTINE OF COMEDIANS JOE WEBER AND
LEW FIELDS — AND SAID TO BE THE FIRST OUTING OF THE GAG.</small>

THEIR ROOTS WERE in Poland — where Fields, a tailor's son, was born in 1867 — and from where Weber's mother, Kosher butcher father and siblings travelled, via Birmingham England, shortly before his birth in New York the same year. Their entirely American success resonated down the twentieth century and across the Atlantic. Their routine was rooted in the experience of the new arrival, the immigrant, and drew on knockabout — "Don't poosh me Meyer!" — and word play, exemplified in Weber's greeting, "I am delightfulness to see you!" and Fields's "The disgust is all mine!" Weber was plump — and padded — Fields thin. Their Double-Dutch act was an archetype, and perfect for New York at the turn of the nineteenth and twentieth centuries.

In 1810 the population of the city's five boroughs had been less than 120,000. By 1900 it was just under three and a half million. Immigrants arrived from China and Italy, Eastern Europe and Ireland, the Ottoman and the Austro-Hungarian Empires. There were Italians clustered around Canal Street, Irish north of 14th Street, African-Americans north of 60th, and more Germans in New York than in any German city apart from Berlin.

New York was even more a city of ethnic communities, demarcated around class, money, and status. The humour of Weber and Fields — "Your family got thrown out on the street so many times that your mother had to buy curtains vot matched the sidewalk" — drew in

a following which reflected, and transcended the divisions.

Joseph Moishe Weber had collided with Moses Schoenfeld when they were both eight, both running away from other kids in the Bowery. The double act debuted soon after, with a blackface routine at a cheap Lower East Side music hall.

By the end of the 1880s they had toured the country and set up Weber and Fields Own Company. Then, in 1896, the lease became available on what was regarded as an ill-starred theatre, the 700-seat Imperial Music Hall on Broadway and 29th Street. There had been hits at the Imperial; Marie Lloyd proclaimed in 1894 in the British music hall paper the *Era* that she had enjoyed "instantaneous success" but her engagement had ended with her being fired by the manager Fred Kraus. Since 1892 Kraus had lost seventy thousand dollars. But it was, Weber and Fields realised, even if few other people did, the right place at the right time.

Union Square, south of the Imperial, was still the focus of the American theatre industry. The Bowery was still a place of cheap dives and singing saloons, whorehouses and music halls, but from the 1880s it was home too for ethnic Italian theatre and for the Yiddish theatre growing out of the eastern European Jewish migration.

But just as Tony Pastor had developed a new variety and moved it out of the Bowery, so others had moved on. Theatres, department stores and the tide of affluent New York had washed beyond Union Square, beyond Madison Square, towards Central Park. The super-rich meanwhile, had advanced to 95th Street, and built French-style chateaux as they went. It was a world of ostentation, cultural elitism, unparalleled conspicuous consumption, and thus a world eminently suitable for parody.

For Weber and Fields the Imperial's location was ideal. It was in the middle of the theatre district, near the Madison Square hotels — and near the "Ladies' Mile". By day this was an upmarket shopping area, by night it was a centre of prostitution, part of the Tenderloin of bordellos and brothels between Fifth and Eighth avenues. The Tenderloin stretched from Koster and Bial's Music Hall at Sixth Avenue and 23rd Street — where Lloyd made her American debut in 1890 —and by 1900 had extended to 50th Street.

The Imperial had lost money while enjoying a sleazy reputation built, unsuccessfully, around the risqué burlesque that had developed since the 1870s in the wake of the more respectable Lydia Thompson and her British Blondes. The Imperial's reputation was transformed with the arrival of Weber and Fields. But the first thing to go was the name.

Three years earlier Charles Frohman had opened his prestigious Empire Theatre, on the edge of what was then Longacre Square. This then marked the furthest move Uptown of the theatre district. The Imperial became Weber and Fields Music Hall. From September 1896 to May 1904 the hall was to be home to a variety style based on comic "travesties" of the hits of "legitimate" theatre, and it was wildly successful, particularly amongst the social class who were parodied.

Then in 1904 Weber and Fields were hit by the occupational hazard of double acts, a series

Weber and Fields: After them — everybody.

of rows. They broke up, and pursued solo careers, including time working as producers. In 1912, they revived their act. Later they continued with their solo careers, made some movies together, worked in radio and resumed producing. Fields died in 1941; Weber in 1942.

Weber had no children, but Fields fathered a show business dynasty. Its members included the lyricist Dorothy Fields, who wrote for Cotton Club reviews in the late 1920s, for Astaire and Rogers in the 1930s — including Jerome Kern's 'The Way You Look Tonight' — and with Cole Porter and Sigmund Romberg. And it was Dorothy who co-wrote the book of *Annie Get Your Gun*. In the 1960s, one hundred years after her father had set out from Poland, she was collaborating with Cy Coleman on *Sweet Charity*.

The secret of his success

The music hall as I remember it was not a place where a man could take his wife. I laid down the principle that given good clean entertainment clean people would come to see it. The man did bring his wife, and that has been the secret of my success.

RICHARD THORNTON.

CHARLES MORTON, TONY Pastor, Richard Thornton; London, New York — and South Shields, a town now of 87,200 souls, perched on the south side of the estuary of the River Tyne, ten miles from Newcastle. There, on a grey afternoon, I go in search of Thornton and his good, clean, lucrative late-nineteenth, early twentieth century enterprise.

South Shields was not a clean place, then, it was no rural market town. There had been four hundred years of salt pans, two hundred years of glass works and the St Hilda Colliery had been producing coal since 1811. There were chemical factories, and there was shipbuilding. Its population was less than nine thousand when Thornton was born there in 1839, but the place was textbook British Industrial Revolution. That year St Hilda's exploded and killed 59 miners —including a nine-year-old boy "driver".

By the time Thornton was that age he was sharpening picks for the mine with his father, and learning the violin. In his teens he was playing at the local beauty spot, the Marsden Grotto, and on the Tyneside leisure boats and in local pubs.

He avoided the pit, working at a local cabinet maker's stores, got married and kept up the music. By 1870 he was the leader of the orchestra at the local Theatre Royal. By the 1880s he was landlord of the Shakespeare Arms in Union Street, "Pig Alley", and there he set up a music room. It flourished, and in 1885 he took over the adjacent land and created what became Thornton's Music Hall. It was the London pattern of the 1850s, rippling across the country.

In the 1860s South Shields' population was recorded as fewer than 10,000, by the 1890s the figure was closer to 100,000, bigger than it is now, and the town was even developing as a seaside resort. Thornton prospered. He took a share in the Theatre Royal in Sunderland from Edward Moss, who had been building a variety theatre chain since the 1870s. Moss had begun at the Gaiety in Edinburgh. By 1885 he had another Gaiety in Newcastle-upon-Tyne, but Moss wanted another theatre in Newcastle. So did Thornton, who bought a failed public house, the Scotch Arms and began turning it into a variety theatre. The two men collaborated and in 1890 came up with the

Empire Palace Newcastle, which survived until the great cull of theatres in the 1960s.

Newcastle and Sunderland were big cities, but Thornton had not finished with South Shields. Thornton's Varieties was still in business and in April 1896 moving pictures arrived. The technology had moved with astounding speed. "Cinematographe" had debuted in Paris in December 1895. It reached London in February 1896, and here it was in South Shields sharing the bill with one hundred (live) local schoolchildren performing *China And Japan*, a pageant presumably inspired by the war then raging between the Chinese and Japanese Empires.

Two years later Thornton knocked down his old variety theatre. In its place came the Empire Palace, with its main entrance on South Shields' grand boulevard, Kings Street. And with that had come a fleeting collaboration between the three architects whose work dominated the British age of the Empires from the 1880s to the 1929 Wall Street crash, Frank Matcham from Devon, and two local brothers, William and Thomas "T.R." Milburn from Sunderland.

The Empire Palace succumbed to the talkies in 1934, and was converted into a cinema. Movies had always had a presence there, and in February 1919 there was an 80th birthday commemoration for Thornton, complete with film of the old man at home.

> **EMPIRE PALACE,**
> KING STREET, SOUTH SHIELDS.
> Proprietors   -   -   The South Shields Empire Palace, Ltd
> Managing Director, Mr. R. Thornton. | General Manager, Mr. Frank Allen
> Resident Manager - Mr. Ernest Bridgen.
>
> **Monday, June 5th, and Twice Nightly During Week**
> G. H. ELLIOTT,
> The Chocolate Coloured Coon.
> **THE KIORYS,**
> Continental Talking Prestidigitateur.
> LITTLE   FREDDY   HACKIN,
> The Phenomenal Boy Comedian.
> SUPPORTED BY A GRAND STAR COMPANY,
> And a Grand Selection of Animated Pictures.
>
> Orch. Stalls 1/-; Circle 9d.; Pit-Stalls 6d.; Pit 4d.;
> Gallery 3d.
>
> **PICTURE MATINEE EVERY WEDNESDAY.**
> PRICES: Orchestral Stalls 6d. Grand Circle 4d.
> Pit Stalls 3d., Pit 2d., Gallery 1d.

That day in King Street I stare at a picture of Thornton in old age, a tough old bird, perched on a bench — suit, boater, wing collar, walrus moustache. Morton went for big side-whiskers, and Pastor favoured a more baroque moustache, but then Morton remained locked in that mid-Victorian era, and Pastor was New York Italian. Thornton is a portrait of an Edwardian, a man who kept it clean, and booked W.C. Fields and G.H. Elliott "the chocolate coloured coon" and Charlie Chaplin and Little Freddy Hackin "the phenomenal boy comedian" and Harry Lauder and the Kiorys "continental talking prestidigateur" on to his North-Eastern Circuit. Thornton looked like Colonel Blimp. According to his friend, the star male impersonator Vesta Tilley, when Thornton moved to Newcastle, and took over the terraced

Eden Villa in Gosforth, he promptly ran into trouble with his neighbours. Impressed by Norway's wooden homes, Thornton had had one installed in Eden Villa's spacious garden, and lived in it. The neighbours complained. Thornton bought the freehold of the terrace, and served notice on his neighbours.

In 1935 the Empire Palace became Black's Regal. In its new incarnation it was opened by a local movie actress, Victoria Hopper, star of *Lorna Doone*, she was supported by the St, Hilda Colliery Band. Later it was the Odeon Regal, then came bingo, then, nothing.

But I know that something is left, but I don't even know where in King Street Thornton's pride and joy is. Well, a newspaper seller tells me, the Odeon was before his time. He directs me to the museum, situated inside a fine and renovated mid-Victorian free library. The lady there sends me on to the local history section, downstairs at the library beyond the shopping mall. There is a fine wind coming up off the Tyne.

History closed around Richard Thornton. The library has a great little local history of South Tyneside cinemas and just two faded cyclostyled newspaper cuttings about him. Almost unreadable, they report that Thornton's fiddle, the instrument that helped save him from St. Hilda's and set him off on his path to Eden Villa, Gosforth, Newcastle-upon-Tyne and a fortune, at death, of £100,000 had been discovered in Sunderland. And the Empire Palace? Left back on to King Street, says the librarian, next to Marks and Spencer.

I would have missed it. But looking for the old halls makes me look up. There, in the pedestrian precinct with Vision Express and W.H. Smith and Woolworth's is New Shoefayre, next to Marks and Spencer. Above the shop is the distinctive Frank Matcham arch, still there, one hundred and seven years on. The glass in the arch has been painted white; someone has etched SAFC, Sunderland Association Football Club into it, colliery bands, football clubs, tribal associations. I walk past the shoe racks marked "all £2" and "75% off". The ladies behind the counter are friendly and helpful, and know little. It all went, said the older lady, her friend says that in the stockroom, well, someone said something about — ghosts? The older lady laughs. No, she says. Nothing there, no ghosts.

But it is still a fine frontage. *The Guide To British Theatres* remarks on the unusual layout. The entrance foyer — where Shoefayre is — was separated from the auditorium "by a narrow street with the stalls reached by a tunnel and the first floor balcony by a bridge". I stand and stare; Thornton wanted the best of both worlds. The Empire Palace occupied the plot where he had built his old variety theatre. By placing the foyer on the main street, he ensured prestige, and situated himself next door to the Theatre Royal, where once he had played first fiddle.

At the Market Place Square, just up from the Empire Palace, only one building survived "a savage attack" in April 1941, by what the local paper called "Nazi Moonlight Raiders". It is the fine, elegant, tiny town hall, which served South Shields from 1768 to 1910. I ascend its stairs and look back down King Street and magic up the crowds outside the Empire and the Theatre Royal. On that night of six thousand incendiaries, the Moonlight Raiders did for South Shields' other theatre, the Queen's, where Old Mother Riley was playing. Curiously the war had already done for the St Hilda Colliery. Its market had been Italy, and with Mussolini's entry into the War, in 1940, it closed forever. Later, the world market would do for South Shields' proud shipbuilding. I walk back past the Empire Palace to what looks depressingly like King Street's modern hub, its Co-op supermarket. There is a hell of a wind off the Tyne.

Sometimes it was a living... The 1900s, and the 'skirt dance'.

More azure than ultramarine

Apart from the vast improvement from the pot house character of the old time halls so the character of the entertainment has been improved almost out of knowledge. For example the so-called "comic" songs of the last century's early seventies, and even the early eighties, often were of the most cerulean character-the tinge being more ultramarine than azure.

CHARLES MORTON, "THE FATHER OF THE HALLS", LOOKING BACK, FROM 1905, ON THE BAD OLD, GOOD OLD, DAYS OF MUSIC HALL.

IT WAS NOT just Oswald Stoll and Edward Moss. There were plenty of theatre entrepreneurs and managers in late Victorian and Edwardian Britain — George Payne and Richard Thornton and Tom Barrasford and Frank Macnaghten, and Stoll and Moss were not even the only ones to get knighted for their efforts. Walter de Frece was so rewarded.

But it is Stoll and Moss whose names outlive those times. Partly because of Stoll's moral code, or prudishness as Sophie Tucker and many others would have put it, and partly because, just as Albee-Keith dominated American vaudeville, so Moss Empires was a symbol of British mass live entertainment which still has a resonance in the twenty-first century.

Moss was the son of a theatre manager and born in 1866 in Ashton-under-Lyne, in Staffordshire. Stoll, an engineer's son, was born in Melbourne Australia in 1866. Three years later he was brought back to Britain by his now widowed mother, a onetime dancer with the "Hardcastle Sisters".

In the late 1870s Moss took over two music halls in Edinburgh. He then added halls in Newcastle-upon-Tyne and Glasgow to his circuit and in 1890 teamed up with Thornton on the Newcastle Empire Palace project. In the ensuing decade there were to be five more Empires. Moss had transformed the Imperial dream — or Indian sales package — of Benjamin Disraeli into a trademark.

Stoll meanwhile had settled with his mother in Liverpool, and in his teens took over the

Oswald Stoll: the teetotal social crediter who created a mass medium (*left*) and one of the outlets in Brighton (*opposite, right*).

Mr Stoll, you shouldn't be the manager of a vaudeville theatre. You should be a bishop.

running of the Parthenon music hall following his stepfather George Stoll's death. By 1890, aged 23, Stoll had taken over Levino's Music Hall in Cardiff and renamed it the Cardiff Empire. It took him seven months to make a profit, but once he had, with his mother employed in the box office, he never looked back.

In 1898 he collaborated with Moss on the Nottingham Empire, and a year later the two men, together with Thornton and his assistant Frank Allen, set up Moss Empires Ltd. It was the turning point. Out of outposts in industrial Wales, Scotland and the north-east, three entrepreneurs had set about the British organisation of variety, from its disreputable

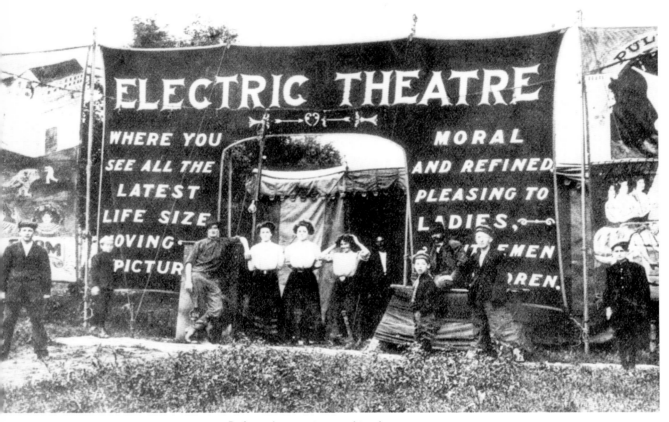

Before the movies got big, they even got tents.
A cinematograph show of the early 1900s.

origins in London, into the modern world's first commercially ruled, regulated and pasteurised mass medium. There was a circuit, there were stars, there were big profits, and there was a strict moral code, for what was said on stage at least. And in 1901 came one of the great, and surviving, London variety theatres, the Frank Matcham-designed Hackney Empire. As managing director of Moss Empires, wrote Stoll's biographer Felix Barker,

Sir Oswald controlled 28 theatres which entertained 90,000 people a day, employed 600 artists and had a pay-roll of more than two thousand people, including his mother, who continued to guest in the box office into the 1920s. But in 1910 Stoll pulled back from Moss Empires to resume independent operation of his own chain. Two years later Moss was dead, but Stoll, teetotal, non-smoking and devoted, unlike the Conservative Moss, to the interwar social credit movement lived on until 1942.

There are various reasons given for the decline and fall of the British Empire and the palaces of varieties and there are many reasons but I often think that it was Sir Oswald with his methods, and without of course any intention of doing it — who was the start of it.

VETERAN VARIETY PERFORMER CLARKSON ROSE.

Plush box draperies and curtains

The prevailing tints were terra-cotta, blue, white and gold, the upholstering and furnishing being very luxurious, with its thick Axminster carpets, plush box draperies and curtains, while the tableaux curtains completed the air of luxury. And so the denizens of boxes, pit, stalls and gallery settled themselves down in unwonted comfort for what was to come…

FROM *A SOUVENIR OF THE EMPIRE THEATRE*. BIRMINGHAM'S EMPIRE PALACE, WHICH OPENED IN MAY 1894, WAS BUILT FOR EDWARD MOSS, DESIGNED BY FRANK MATCHAM, BOMBED AND DESTROYED BY FIRE IN OCTOBER 1940.

ARCHITECT FRANK MATCHAM worked on Birmingham's Empire Palace during the high tide of his spectacular career. During that decade, for Edward Moss the variety entrepreneur, Matcham produced the first Moss Empire, Edinburgh's Empire Palace in 1892, the Sheffield Empire in 1895, the Cardiff Empire in 1896 — for Oswald Stoll — the Glasgow Empire in 1897, the Leeds Empire in 1898, and that year too, working for Moss and Oswald Stoll together, the Empire Palace in Nottingham. Of that particular crop, only one, in Edinburgh, survives. It is now the Festival Theatre, and was completely rebuilt in 1928 by the Sunderland architects William and T.R. Milburn, with whom Matcham had collaborated on the Empire Palace in South Shields in 1898.

In Britain, between the 1870s and the outbreak of the First World War, Matcham was the original architect on at least eighty theatres and did extensive work on as many again. He was popular with show business moguls and with the public, but less so with critics at the time. But the arguments that his detractors advanced against him, including his wild eclecticism, have boomeranged. In the last forty years it is just that wonderful mixture of inspirations which has provided much of the case for Matcham.

Often working with the great theatre decorator Felix de Jong, who provided plasterwork and paintings, Matcham was the genius behind the look of the golden era of British variety. It was a look based on creative plundering.

Matcham had a peculiar sense for the imperial dreams of late-Victorian England. The Victorian subconscious had roamed continental Europe and gone beyond, to summon up visions of a mysterious, Moorish-Islamic east captured in everything from the art of Sir Henry Alma-Tadema to the novels (and politics) of Benjamin Disraeli. With Matcham they resurfaced in the bricks, mortar, plaster and paint of theatres. There was baroque, nymphs, shepherds and cherubs, lustrous gold and deep scarlet, arches, burnished domes and golden corridors. This was a world that had definitively broken with singing saloons, pleasure gardens and penny gaffs. This was a world where the money of the hundreds of thousands of new customers, filtered through the cash-tills of Edward Moss, Richard Thornton and Oswald Stoll, turned into palaces for the common people, illuminated by the goddess Electra, for gas illumination was beginning to give way to the new technology of electricity.

Matcham, the son of a brewery manager, was born in Newton Abbot in Devon in 1854, and

"Architect Matcham."

educated in Torquay. At the age of fourteen he joined the office of a local architect, George Bridgeman, and five years later came his first theatre — he was Bridgeman's assistant at Paignton in Devon on the Oldway House. In the mid–1870s Matcham joined the practice of the London architect Jethro Robinson, who had a substantial involvement in theatre work.

Robinson also had two daughters. Matcham married Maria, the youngest, and on her father's death in 1878, becoming head of the family business, he completed Robinson's work on the Elephant and Castle theatre. The brisk trickle of work turned into a torrent as the century ended, climaxing with buildings like the Hackney Empire in 1901, and Oswald Stoll's expensive pride and joy, the London Coliseum, in 1904.

The torrent had ebbed by 1914. Matcham's last Empire was in Wood Green, in north London. But he continued to work on cinemas, pubs, and other designs. And, out on the River Thames at Tagg's Island, he designed Fred Karno's Kasino, a short-lived monument for the comedy impresario who had helped launch the career of Charlie Chaplin. His end was sudden and bizarre; he cut his finger — and died of blood poisoning in 1920.

Frank Matcham: a beard of his time, ahead of his time.

Storm and stress

If many of us fall back under storm and stress, the struggle will be prolonged. But I can boldly declare, and with certainty, that so long as there is even a handful of men true to their pledge, there can only be one end to the struggle and that is victory.

MAHATMA GANDHI, SPEAKING AT THE EMPIRE PALACE OF VARIETIES, JOHANNESBURG, SOUTH AFRICA, 1906.

BARNETT ISAACS WAS his name at first. He was born in 1852, in Aldgate in London. As a teenager, he played straight man to his older brother Harry on the London music halls. It was then that the siblings decided on a change of name. It was an era of Os on the halls, Tom Costello, Sam Mayo, Dan Leno, the Conjuror Bosco — and so exit Barnett enter Barney Barnato, future diamond dealer, financier and, always, East End chancer. In 1873 Barney followed Harry to Kimberley South Africa, the diamond rush and the road to a fortune. Councillor Barnato, using the patter of the halls, seduced Kimberley's local authority, Mayor Barnato sewed up the town for the new rich, briber Barnato bought justice, multi-millionaire Barnato consorted and conspired with Cecil Rhodes and Paul Kruger, built a racecourse — and invested in the one-time Globe Theatre Johannesburg.

In 1893 the Globe was transformed into the Empire Palace of Varieties and it became known as the "Jewish theatre". Three years later South Africa's first film show was staged at the Empire; in 1897 came a tour by the most famous East Ender in the world, and a friend of Barnato, Marie Lloyd. She played to packed houses.

Nine years later, after the wars between the British Empire and the Boers, the Empire was packed again. A succession of outraged South African Indian speakers, including a 37-year-old Indian-born lawyer, Mohandas Gandhi, were denouncing the "Asiatic Law Amendment" which required all Indians over the age of eight to be fingerprinted and carry a pass. This was being introduced by the Transvaal government — with the collusion of the British.

The key, unanimous resolution at the Empire meeting was the fourth, pledging before God, to take any penalty rather than surrender to the "Black Amendment". The meeting, which ended with the singing of 'God Save The King', was a seminal moment in the development of Gandhian non-violence.

In 1915 Gandhi left South Africa forever. The fruits of that day in 1906 would be gathered at midnight on August 14, 1947, with the independence of India, and, in South Africa, on February 11, 1990, with the release of Nelson Mandela.

A few hours after that 1906 meeting the Empire Palace of Varieties was destroyed by fire. As for Barney Barnato, he missed that moment. Soon after Marie Lloyd's South African debut he had taken the SS *Scott* from Cape Town for Southampton, en route for Queen Victoria's 1897 Diamond Jubilee. Mentally unbalanced, he flung himself into the sea south of Madeira, and drowned.

Ragtime and the pink hat

…In the view of the Constitution, in the eye of the law, there is in this country no superior, dominant, ruling class of citizens. There is no caste here. Our constitution is color-blind, and neither knows nor tolerates classes among citizens. In respect of civil rights, all citizens are equal before the law… The destinies of the two races, in this country are indissolubly linked together, and the interest of both require that the common government of all shall not allow the seeds of race hate to be planted under the sanction of law. What can more certainly arouse race hate, what can more certainly create a feeling of distrust between these races, than state enactments, which, in fact, proceed on the ground that colored citizens are so inferior and degraded that they cannot be allowed to sit in public coaches occupied by white citizens?

JOHN MARSHALL HARLAN, ASSOCIATE JUSTICE OF THE UNITED STATES SUPREME COURT, DISSENTING FROM WHAT HE CALLED THE "PERNICIOUS" RULING OF THE SUPREME COURT IN THE PLESSEY VERSUS FERGUSON CASE THAT THE DOCTRINE OF "SEPARATE BUT EQUAL" WAS NOT DISCRIMINATORY, MAY 1896.

ONE DAY, RESEARCHING *Lost Empires*, looking for something else, I am reading *The Times*, autumn and winter, 1905. That November the refurbished Empire Leicester Square reopened. Two performances, at 2.15pm and 8.15pm, were advertised of a new ballet *divertissement*, a revue entitled "Rogues and Vagabonds", Professor Bernar's Marionettes, Mr. W. Louis Bradfield, Biograph Pictures (seeds of music hall destruction) — and then there were The Brittons.

A *Times* reviewer is impressed by the show. As for The Brittons, they came on at about half past ten. They were, he says, "an exhilarating pair of negro dancers and singers". I am intrigued.

Blacks are part of British theatre at least back into the eighteenth century, that I know. In the United States there are black acts and actors, back to colonial times, back to Ira Aldridge and James Hewlitt from the 1820s and 1840s who crossed the Atlantic to ply their trade. The incredible Thomas Grimes, "Blind Tom", onetime slave, concert and vaudeville star, composer and pianist could play just about anything, flawlessly, and, having been systematically ripped off by a series of white "managers" died at fifty-nine, in 1908, after a half-century long career. There was the "African Nightingale", the soprano Elizabeth Taylor Greenfield in mid-nineteenth century, the comedians Billy Kersands and Bert Williams in the late nineteenth and early twentieth century and the list goes on for ever.

And then there was ragtime and that 1896 Supreme Court ruling. White supremacists were back in power in the south, and the south had its fingers back clutching the windpipe of the Union. Plessey versus Ferguson, the case of a black man being thrown out of a "whites only" railway carriage in New Orleans, was just icing on the cake. But it codified racism in the US for half a century.

"Mr Britton," says *The Times* reviewer, "is a gentleman of much courtesy, combined with a signal power of shaking the leg and tapping the foot..." So, sixty years before, the great American dancer William Henry "Juba" Lane, had been seen and lauded by Charles Dickens. In the 1840s, Lane had played London's Vauxhall Gardens.

Plessey versus Ferguson coincided with the explosion of ragtime into dance halls, vaudeville and music halls, first in the United States, then around the world. Ragged time, the first African-American-rooted music to flood into the mainstream on anything remotely like its own terms, intermingling with white forms, filterered, refined, born in the nurseries of modern popular music, brothels, cheap saloons, and bars.

In *The Times*, a few weeks before the Empire review, downpage, was a story about a Mr George Plimpton, late of the *Chicago Tribune*, compiler of lynching statistics. He

Scott Joplin, king of ragtime. It would be the 1970s before his act got a reprise.

reckoned that the rate was falling. No matter, it would rise again. In 1904, the paper said, "out of eighty-seven persons killed, eighty-three were coloured. Forty were lynched for actual or attempted murder and twenty for actual or attempted assault on women." That was the great thing about lynching, no worries about evidence or due process. In a further nineteen cases cause was put down simply as "race prejudice".

The "king of the ragtime writers", Scott Joplin, was born in east Texas and grew up in Texarkana. His father was an African-American labourer and former slave, his free-born mother a domestic servant. Taught in childhood by a German immigrant musician, Joplin absorbed European influences into his music. In the ensuing years Joplin lived and practised in Sedalia Missouri — which had a thriving black community and where he studied at college — and St Louis. By the time Joplin published 'Original Rags' and the 'Maple Leaf Rag' in 1899, the music was already well established; Joplin's rivals included the sixteen-year-old Baltimore-born pianist Eubie Blake, who wrote his 'Charleston Rag', one of the first of more than two thousand compositions, that year.

'Maple Leaf Rag' was to sell more than half a million copies in sheet music within a decade. Ragtime was technology; cheap sheet music, pianola player-pianos, and, via the phonograph, recorded sound. The old verities of western popular music had gone. But while, in the first fifteen years of the twentieth century, Joplin published more than three dozen rags, and wrote two operas, neither of which were properly performed in his lifetime, and a symphony, his work did not provide *the* big hit.

Come on and hear
Alexander's Ragtime Band,
Come on and hear,
It's the best band in the land!
They can play a bugle call
Like you never heard before,
So natural that you want to go to war
That's just the bestest band what am,
Honey lamb!

FROM IRVING BERLIN'S 'ALEXANDER'S RAGTIME BAND', 1911

The week The Brittons played the Empire *The Times* was reporting on the first Russian revolution. The Tsar's very own proto-fascists, the Black Hundreds, had launched "wholesale massacres of the Jews" around Odessa in the south-west Ukraine — and the Jews had fought back.

At that time, at the Pelham Café in New York's Chinatown, the Siberian-born son of a cantor, sixteen-year-old Israel Baline, was making out as a singing waiter. He wrote his first song two years later, and changed his name. Thus it was in 1911, as Irving Berlin, that he wrote, and performed 'Alexander's Ragtime Band'. Strictly speaking it wasn't a rag, but, played in Empires, Hippodromes and the Imperial trenches of the First World War, it defined the era. Jews, out of the Russian Empire's bloodbath, headed for western Europe, the United States, hope and creativity.

Berlin, the man who became New York and American music, died at the age of one hundred and one in 1989. Joplin, rediscovered in the 1970s, died, aged forty-nine or fifty, of *dementia paralytica* — syphilis — in 1917. Blake, a man whose works included 'I'm Just Wild About Harry', and whose principles ensured that there would be no racist compromises or "blackface" routines in his career, died, aged one hundred, in 1983.

"Mrs (or Miss) Britton," continues *The Times's* reviewer, "wears a pink hat of monstrous size, and dances as if she were made of steel springs and gutta percha." It was the pink hat that gets to me, wonderful, magnificent, a pink cloud I reckon, floating on Ms Britton's head, as she transfixes her audience, transcends time.

"Together," the reviewer concludes, "they are an amusing and inspiriting pair." Still are. I think a lot about The Brittons, who they were, where they went, one of those thousands of acts that came on at ten thirty, lit up the stage, and disappeared back into the alleys off Leicester Square, hidden from history. A black act from that time when jazz, unique American art, was germinating. I think of The Brittons, and I think six decades down the century, of Southampton's sometime Empire, of the early 1960s, and me, catching up with Coleman Hawkins, Roy Eldridge, Ella Fitzgerald, and Irving Berlin: 'How Deep Is The Ocean?'

Noble Sissle (*left*) and Eubie Blake (*right*). Their musical partnership began in 1915 — and revived in the early 1950s.

Why fear death?

Having once seen a theatre, he never saw anything else.

THE PLAYWRIGHT J.M. BARRIE, THE CREATOR OF *PETER PAN*, ON THE PRODUCER CHARLES FROHMAN.

The sinking of the *Lusitania* in 1915 (*top*) and thus the end of Charles Frohman (*right*).

THERE WERE THREE Frohman brothers, Gustave, Daniel and Charles, sons of Henry Frohman, a German immigrant peddler, who arrived in the United States in 1845, and settled in Ohio. When Charles was four, Henry moved his family to New York. All three brothers entered show business, all had a hand in creating stars, but only one, Charles, created an Empire, "the star factory" as well.

Frohman's theatre opened in 1893. It was at 1430 Broadway, just below 40th Street. Even by its location, it created a revolution, because the Empire was then the furthest north of Manhattan's theatres, just south of the nondescript Longacre Square. In the ensuing decade, everything changed. New York's most fashionable restaurants either opened, or — like Delmonico's in 1898 — moved to the area. Three years later, electricity took over Broadway, and the "Great White Way" began dazzling the world. Then in 1902, with the arrival of the *New York Times* tower on Longacre Square, Times Square was born. Theatre moved Uptown in the wake of the Empire.

Born in 1860, Frohman was introduced to theatre when he was eight. It was America's first musical, *The Black Crook*, at Niblo's Pleasure Garden on Lower Broadway, and he sold programmes. By the time he was fourteen he was selling tickets at Hooley's Theatre in Brooklyn and plugging minstrel shows for his brother Gustave. In 1883 he opened his first production, the melodrama *The Stranglers Of Paris*, and his own office, at 1215 Broadway. He was working as an agent, a road manager, and, most of all, an enthusiastic producer. Then he took on Bronson Howard's play *Shenandoah*. It had been badly reviewed in Boston in 1888. It was about the Civil War, it was long, Frohman organized a partial rewrite, and raised the money for an 1889 New York production at the Star Theatre.

Frohman never looked back. By 1890 he had set about organizing a stock company, was recruiting a group of actors who either were stars — like William Gillette with whom the teenage Charlie Chaplin was to work — or were to become stars under Frohman's tutelage. Then came the Empire Theatre, and in 1896 the Theatrical Syndicate by which, for twenty years, a small cartel carved up the nation's theatres, and through which Frohman developed his stars — and his plays.

The Empire became famous, or infamous, for the number of European, and particularly British, plays it imported. Through Frohman the likes of Oscar Wilde and J.M. Barrie got early productions in New York, and thanks to Frohman's encouragement, Barrie's *Peter Pan* got produced in London, and in New York. And Frohman also went the other way. He produced plays in Paris and opened offices in Henrietta Street in Covent Garden. Moving into London's theatreland, he at various stages controlled the Duke of York's, where *Peter Pan* premiered, the Globe, the Vaudeville, the Comedy — and the Empire.

Then, in 1915, he boarded the liner *Lusitania* for a trip to London, to meet Barrie. The ship was torpedoed, and Frohman drowned. His last words echoing the boy who wouldn't grow up, were, claimed a survivor: "Why fear death? It is the most beautiful adventure of life."

Even a whisper was never lost

The Empire is so dear to me it is difficult to speak of her. It seems almost like praising one's mother. She was always such a kind theatre and so friendly. She never took one's words and stuffed them away in corners; even a whisper was never lost, and an actor felt that there was a friend in front, helping and sustaining him… May she look forward to another fifty years of faithful service.

MAUDE ADAMS CELEBRATING BROADWAY'S EMPIRE THEATRE ON ITS FIFTIETH BIRTHDAY IN 1943.

THE BEAUTIFUL, ENIGMATIC Maude Adams has slipped into history now. But once, a century ago, there was no bigger American stage star, on tour for Charles Frohman around the United States, and, back in New York, at Frohman's Empire. It had been at the Empire, in 1897-98, that Adams achieved fame, giving three hundred performances in J.M Barrie's *The Little Minister*. On the show's last night, displaying, yet again, his talent for promotion, Frohman presented every woman in the audience with an American Beauty rose.

The Empire on Broadway was not as other Empires. The Empires of Britain might trade in cheap variety, turns, music hall and dancing girls. Frohman's half-a-million-dollars-worth of Empire was drama, on and off the stage. Its first production David Belasco and Franklin Fyles' *The Girl I Left Behind Me* was a genteel comedy set on an army outpost in Montana. It was aimed at, and got, the carriage trade. Describing opening night in 1893, Frohman's publicity machine wrote of "fair women in rich cloaks and jewels", ushers in full evening dress. and, inside, the "rare marbles of the wainscotings, the agates and onyx in the stiles and pilasters, the foliated borders and garlanded friezes" which "made a brilliant and delight-giving ensemble."

A charisma that transcends time,
Maude Adams.

up, and by and large it did.

The lynchpin of that system in the early days was the actor John Drew, the son of an Irish-born actor father, an actress mother and not only the precursor of a dynasty but a man who traced his thespian roots back to Elizabethan strolling players. It was after Drew opened, with Maude Adams, in Louis N. Parker and Murray Carson's play *Rosemary* on August 31, 1896 that the Empire really took off. And each year around Labor Day Drew would open in a new, largely forgettable play at the theatre. Not only was his performance assessed, but his style was too. What Drew wore became fashion, just as the saying of the era was "the season opens when John Drew opens at the Empire".

Amongst the cast members in *Rosemary* was Drew's niece, Ethel Barrymore. She had debuted, aged 15, in 1894, in another Drew vehicle, *The Bauble Shop*. Her brothers were Lionel and John. Drew's great-grand-niece, in the twenty-first century, is Drew Barrymore.

Rosemary was Adams's last double act with Drew. Frohman took her off to make her a solo star. She starred in seven J.M. Barrie plays including, in 1905, *Peter Pan*. Adams became the first, and definitive, American interpreter of the boy who wouldn't grow up, and it was a role that she was to play more than 1500 times. Out of the Empire she became, it was said, a woman who could fill any theatre in the United States, and earning $20,000 a week, was probably the best-paid stage actress in the world. Then, in 1918, she effectively retired. There was a scatter of other performances, and in 1937 she set up the drama department at Stephen's College in Colombia Missouri, taught there until 1950 and largely lived with her friend Louise Boynton.

A decade later Frohman had the theatre completely renovated, in the style of Louis XIV, as reinterpreted in the New York in the age of the robber barons. And that was the Empire that became the last survivor of New York's Victorian theatres.

The Empire at the turn of the nineteenth and twentieth centuries, and for many years after, was likened to an American version of the Comédie Français. Belasco and a few others aside, most of the plays were transatlantic imports — Frohman, visited Europe every year — and central to their success was the producer's promotion of the star system. The play might be lousy, and many were, but, reasoned Frohman, if the names in lights were big enough, then the audience would show

On this spot

One cold day in the New York Fall I go looking for lost Imperials and
Empires, Maude Adams and John Drew. There are plenty of out-of-towners,
me included, around Times Square. They are failing to find celebrities at the
Ed Sullivan Theatre, home to David Letterman, on Broadway at 53rd and
54th, queuing for movies, watching buskers and eating.

I check out the eighty-year old Imperial Theatre, on West 45th and West
46th, sandwiched between the Music Box, a six-storey car park and an
electronics shop. The Imperial is dark, as they say, or was that day with
"Hugh Jackman in *The Boy From Oz*" closed and no new show then on the
horizon. The Imperial boasts a dreary frontage, but an impressive auditorium
I am told, but I never got to see it. I rang the doorbell, and after a long
silence, came a scratchy voice. No, she said, no one here, there is no one left.

It was Uptown then, I remind myself, as I head towards Broadway and
40th Street. The crowds have vanished;
strange how fast New York can become
a ghost town. Back in the 1890s the
Empire was opposite the Opera House
— Tchaikovsky appeared there in 1893
— the destruction of which New
Yorkers have been regretting for the
best part of half a century. The Empire
and the Opera must have looked fine
together, but it takes me a while to
figure out where it should have been.

The death sentence was announced
in the New York papers in 1952. I read
a press cutting about it:

"M. Lowenstein & Sons,
manufacturers of integrated cotton and
textiles, announced yesterday that the
firm will construct an eighteen-storey
office building on the ground now
occupied by the Empire Theater, and
the south-east corner of Broadway and
40th Street.

"The famous old Broadway house...
will be razed in the near future", the
textile firm's announcement said. "The
playhouse, which most recently housed

The Empire New
York in the long
season of John Drew.

John Van Druten's play *I Am A Camera* would have celebrated its sixtieth birthday Jan.25, 1953."

Well, the Empire did make sixty. Its last show wasn't *Camera* — *Cabaret's* progenitor — but Arthur Laurent's *The Time Of The Cuckoo*, with Shirley Booth. It closed on May 30, 1953. "Throughout the world," wrote Booth in that week's programme, "actors will join us in our fond farewell, from the Lunts in London to Ina Claire and Ethel Barrymore in California. On tour, Katherine Cornell and Helen Hayes will surely pause on that evening to recall their glories at the Empire, and in Tannersville, New York, the legendary Maude Adams may well re-live her first flight from the Empire's rafters as the original boy who wouldn't grow up — Peter Pan."

The Lowensteins did get their block, all eighteen storeys of it, anonymous, black, grey with 1430 etched out in gold, and a plaque for Steinberg & Pokoik Management Corp. It is a terrible lifeless place, with a Duane Reade on the corner and a nice guy on reception, at the end of the vast echoing foyer, who says, yes, he did know that once there had been a theatre, and indeed, there is a memorial to it just inside the front door.

I retrace my steps. The memorial was erected, it says, by M. Lowenstein & Sons Inc. in 1964.

"On this spot," it announces, "stood the Empire Theatre (1893-1953) made famous by the management of Charles Frohman and these distinguished artists who among many others enriched this theatre's history."

A long list follows. There is Maude, of course, and Judith Anderson, and Margaret Anglin, and the Barrymores, Sarah Bernhardt, Jeanne Eagels, William Gillette, Gertrude Lawrence, Helen Hayes, Leslie Howard, Otis Skinner, Marie Tempest, Ellen Terry....

I stare at it for a while, then walk out into the dusk. Maybe Maude did make her flight that night. Anyway, three months later 80-year-old Maude Ewing Kiskadden Adams from Salt Lake City Utah, later of New York and the Empire, died on her farm.

Maude Adams as Peter Pan (*left*); a theatrical dynasty, Lionel and Ethel Barrymore (*above*) and the last programme for the Empire New York (*below*).

The Farewell Week
PLAYBILL
for The Empire Theatre

THE TIME OF THE CUCKOO

Double act

Nothing would stop him, and he stopped at nothing.
From *Variety's* 1930 obituary of Edward F. Albee.

In Britain entrepreneurs like Moss, Stoll and Thornton cleaned up both the content, and the vast takings of British variety and music hall. Across the Atlantic, the same job was done at the same time by B.F. Keith and his long-time partner, and then successor, Edward F. Albee. They cleaned up a continent by mixing moralising and money so successfully that, by the late 1920s, the Keith-Albee-Orpheum Organisation, set up in 1912, had a stake in four hundred and fifty theatres and controlled the booking of more than seven hundred. It was not a trick that had made either Albee or his partner — who died in 1914 — popular with show business unions, or with their commercial rivals, but then popularity was not what their show was about.

American vaudeville peaked between the 1890s and the end of the 1920s. Its summit coincided with the time that the medium that would kill it — moving pictures — first flickered into life. Indeed Albee and Keith started showing movies in their theatres from 1896, often as "chasers", a cheap way to wrap the shows' live performances. Vaudeville's success was the success, on stage, of a world of internal combustion engines, skyscrapers, Dreadnought battleships, America's manifest destiny and vast, anonymous cities — by 1900 New York's population was approaching three and a half million. Show business might reek of nostalgic references to old ways, old countries and old folk but references were all they were; vaudeville was about the spectacular and the modern, a place of ragtime, erotic dancers like Eva Tanguay — the exception that proved Albee and Keith's moral rules — and pre-packaged touring shows.

Keith was born in Hillsboro Bridge in New Hampshire in 1846. In 1863 he moved to New York, worked fleetingly for Phineas Barnum, served on a steamer plying the east coast trade, and, in 1873 married a devout Catholic. By 1885 he was running his own version of vaudeville at the Bijou Theatre in Boston and had finally fallen in with Albee, eleven years his junior, from Maine, who had been touring with circuses. It was Albee who introduced a bargain basement production of Gilbert and Sullivan's *The Mikado* to the Bijou, which made money, and enabled Keith to begin his expansion. In 1893 came a symbolic moment; Keith moved into the heart of what was still New York's theatreland, and took over the Union Square Theatre. Tony Pastor had cleaned up vaudeville in New York; for Keith and Albee that city was just one stop on a triumphal progress. By 1906 theirs was the United States' largest vaudeville group.

And just as the "Syndicate" was attempting to become the cartel running straight theatre, so in 1900 Keith and Albee were behind the Association of Vaudeville Managers, and six years later they set up the United Booking Office of America, and soon after that a stooge union for variety artists.

In 1916, four years after Keith's death, Albee, having vanquished his business rivals, took on the White Rats, the vaudeville artists union. Their strike and their organisation were ruthlessly, albeit expensively, smashed. Gradually, in the 1920s the organisation began to erode, just as Albee aged. In 1928 Joseph P. Kennedy, the businessman, bootlegger and father of the future president John F. Kennedy, headed a group which won a takeover battle for the group, out of which was to evolve Radio Keith Orpheum, and thus RKO Radio Pictures. Albee was forced into lucrative Florida retirement, but came back, one day, to offer his business thoughts to the patriarch of the Kennedy clan. "Didn't you know, Ed," retorted Kennedy, "you're washed up. You're through." Ed died on March 11, 1930 at a hotel in Palm Beach.

A Bronx tale

ONE SUNDAY, I run out of time, and daylight. I have to leave New York, and I want to find what there might be of this other Empire. The theatre is a mystery. There is a web mention of a place that opened in the mid-1890s, seated 1,660 people, a fair-sized theatre, for the time, a big theatre. By then vaudeville was going out to meet the populations of the boroughs that weren't Manhattan. Theatres were going up in Brooklyn, there was even development in the Bronx. Soon Albee and Keith, swallowing the Orpheum, would move in. Until the late nineteenth century the Bronx had a population below 200,000. There was still farming, and village life turning into park, zoo and open space and by the time that Empire arrived, the elevated railway had got to 131st Street. The Irish and Germans were being joined by Italians and Serbians and Croats and eastern European Jews. There was the Hub, at 149th Street and Third Avenue, as a focus with shops and the Metropolis Theatre in 1904 and the Bronx Opera House in 1913. But this Empire was on Westchester Avenue near East 161st Street.

A century later the Bronx's population had passed one million and the south Bronx, starved of money and hope, became a synonym for urban collapse.

The Bronx is reviving now, but at dusk that day when I take the subway up to Yankee Stadium, and get completely lost, it doesn't look that way. It was the wrong subway stop, and without a local, from Puerto Rico, I wouldn't have found the bus that drops me into a place where the urban world slams into reverse. I walk up from the intersection past scrubby grass and a huge, busted truck to the corner where Colony Fried Chicken is doing good trade. And there I find where Westchester Avenue meets East 161st Street, but alas, nothing but a hole in the ground. Over the street is the Olympic Theatre and Concert Hall but that too is closed. Some Empires die of property speculation, but this Empire, which by the 1940s had given up vaudeville, just died of neglect, I guess. I take the subway back to Manhattan.

Abstruse — but interesting

In the London music halls there is a certain satirical or sceptical attitude towards the commonplace, there is an attempt to turn it inside out, to distrust it somewhat, to point up the illlogicality of the everyday. Abstruse — but interesting.

VLADIMIR LENIN, REVOLUTIONARY, FOUNDER OF THE SOVIET UNION, WRITING TO THE RUSSIAN WRITER MAXIM GORKY, 1907.

"I DEFY ANYONE," suggested the Edwardian caricaturist and writer Max Beerbohm, "not to have loved Dan Leno at first sight. The moment he capered on, with that air of wild determination, squirming in every limb with some deep grievance that must be outpoured, all hearts were his."

Some people defied Beerbohm. Leno was a comedian who dominated British music hall from the 1890s until his death in 1904. Assessing his pantomime double act with Herbert Campbell, the Irish playwright George Bernard Shaw wrote of his "stumblings and wanderings through barren acres of gag". And when Leno played New York in 1897 — unhelpfully billed as the "funniest man on Earth" — one paper charitably said he was "just the kind of Englishman you would naturally think would appeal to Englishmen."

The genius of Leno lay in an English surrealism. In his era it took in Lewis Carroll and Edward Lear and worked on down the twentieth century, in and out of the Empires, on to radio and into television. Its essence was an improvisation about a world — typified by Imperial and post-Imperial English society — which seemed immutable, and therefore was best approached in fantasy and dream. What Leno had, said *The Times*, was a "readiness of invention". Leno took audiences into his confidence through layers of improvisation around characters and situations.

Born George Galvin in St Pancras, central London, in 1860, his parents sang and acted in the halls, and he debuted with them aged four at the Cosmotheca in Paddington; later he settled in Liverpool with his mother and stepfather. At twenty, in Leeds, he won the world clog-dancing championship; six years later he quit the family act, and by the late 1880s he was a star. By the end of the century he even, fleetingly, had his own *Dan Leno's Comic Journal*. But early in the new century drink and mental instability were overcoming him. By 1904, he was dead, the likely cause — concealed at the time — was tertiary syphilis.

Light across a century: Dan Leno (*above and left*) and
an English surrealism.

I always stand at corners, because then I catch them both ways. A fine young fellow came up to me and said, "Governor, will I do for a soldier?" I said "I think so!" I walked round him, and I noticed he walked round at the same time. When I got him before the doctor, the doctor said, "Smirks! you do find them," and then we discovered he'd only one arm. Well, I'd never noticed it because, you see, he kept the arm behind him he hadn't got.

FROM DAN LENO'S SKETCH, *THE RECRUITING SERGEANT*.

Knocked about a bit

…It's a bit of a ruin that Cromwell knocked about a bit
One of the ruins that Cromwell knocked about a bit
In the gay old days, there used to be some doings
No wonder that the poor old abbey went to ruin.

Those that study history
Sing and shout a bit
And you can bet your life there isn't a doubt of it
Outside the Oliver Cromwell, last Saturday night
I was one of the ruins that Cromwell knocked about a bit.

'IT'S A BIT OF A RUIN' (1920) BY HARRY BEDFORD AND TERRY SULLIVAN.

ON TUESDAY OCTOBER 3 1922 Marie Lloyd was performing at the Edmonton Empire in north-east London. She had not been well during her performance at the first house, and looked drawn and ill. A doctor was summoned. He told her to abandon her scheduled second performance. She ignored his advice. "It was the *I Pagliacci* business again," the Empire's manager, Leon Pollack, told *The Times* newspaper.

Marie Lloyd went back on stage, and started into 'It's A Bit Of A Ruin', a late success in her spectacular career. During the song, Pollack explained, Marie had to imitate the "staggering and clumsy buffoonery of a drunken woman". The audience, unaware of her condition — she had been administered drugs — assumed she was providing another example of comic acting. She fell on the stage, amidst shrieks of laughter from the auditorium. She staggered to her feet, collapsed backstage and died the following Saturday.

She was just 52. The Anglo-American poet T.S. Eliot wrote that her death was "a significant moment in English history". The writer, caricaturist and archetypal Edwardian Max Beerbohm observed that of all the women of the Victorian era the three best remembered were Queen Victoria, Florence Nightingale — and Marie Lloyd. Writing in 1999 Marie's latest biographer, Midge Gillies, pointed out that, "of the three, Marie was the only one who spanned the Victorian and Edwardian eras and the Great War".

Matilda Alice Victoria Wood was born in Hoxton in 1870, just a few months before the death of Charles Dickens. Hoxton bordered on the worst slums in Britain and her father was an artificial flower maker, and part-time waiter at the nearby Eagle public house off the City Road. Attached to the pub was the Grecian Music Hall, where, forty years earlier, the mid-Victorian classic, 'Villikins And His Dinah', had first been sung and it was there, in 1884, that Marie made her debut.

Her rise was meteoric, and problems within her marriages, marked by violence, meant that she was an early victim of the effects of massive press coverage. Her performances were marked by humour, perfect pitch and rhythm, a genius for the ad lib — and splendid diction. Some of her songs — like 'Don't Dilly Dally (My Old Man Said Follow The Van)' remain part of the culture of England, just as her stage personality shaped the work of generations of performers.

Marie's background was not that of the secure working class, just as what she often sang about, and joked about, and commented on was uncertainty, the black farce of life for the poor in the huge new metropolises of the modern world. She was not a joiner, but she took an extremely prominent — and well-photographed — part in the 1907 Variety Artists Federation strike.

Most of all she worked. She toured the English-speaking world — and was nearly deported from the United States in 1913 on concocted charges under the White Slave Act. Within Britain, she was the star at the Coliseums, Hippodromes and Empires of the land, from Hackney to Cardiff, Islington to Edinburgh, as music hall reached its zenith, and began its decline. During the Great War she performed in factories and military camps, for which she received no official recognition.

One place she did not get to was the Palace Theatre in London on July 1, 1912. That was the night of the first *Royal Command Variety Performance*, when, according to Oswald Stoll, the mastermind of the Empire theatres, the "Cinderella of the arts" went to the ball at last. Amongst more than one hundred and forty

A revolutionary act and a revolutionary mode of transport.

performers were Vesta Tilley, Harry Lauder and Florrie Forde — but no Marie Lloyd. "Coarseness and vulgarity," said Stoll, were not allowed. Lloyd's response was her own series of "command performances by order of the British public".

An aspect of great charm

To what a beautiful and lordly pleasure house the King and Queen came! The house in Shaftesbury Avenue has always been looked upon as one of the most magnificent in Europe, but the fine architectural features of the building, decorated as they were with thousands of roses, bore an aspect of great charm. The coup d'oeil *from the centre of the stalls to the roof was of a floral fairyland, a fit habitat indeed for Terpsichore, Euterpe and Thalia.*

THE MUSIC HALL PAPER *THE ERA* ON THE INAUGURAL *ROYAL COMMAND VARIETY PERFORMANCE* ON JULY 1, 1912.

FRANK MATCHAM BUILT the first Moss Empire in Edinburgh in 1892, and it was there, in the summer of 1911, that the first *Royal Command Variety Performance* was scheduled, to coincide with the coronation visit of King George V. But then fire devastated the theatre — and killed ten people. So the venue was shifted to London, in July 1912. Two of the greatest music hall stars, Albert Chevalier and Marie Lloyd, had been omitted, but the rest of the acts were the cream of British variety talent. Their appearance coincided with the high tide of the British Empire, and, indeed, the high tide of variety.

World wars and royal mourning aside that show has been a fixture in the British social calendar ever since, albeit one that has been hammered by critics as the tastes, and the cast-list, of the Royal Family have changed, aged and evolved. Not so in 1912, according to *The Era*. The attitude of George V towards the show was "a sheer delight to watch".

More than one hundred and forty artistes took part. There was Pavlova with the Imperial Russian Ballet; the Palace Girls' *A Fantasy In Black And White* and George Robey's 'The Mayor Of Mudcumdyke'; Harry Lauder's

'Roamin' In The Gloamin' and Harry Tate's 'Motoring' sketch. Most of all the show signalled that, whatever the content, respectability had become a star act. Instead of the Prince of Wales's anonymous mid-Victorian visits to Evans's Supper Rooms, a cross-section of the British franchise of Europe's Imperial royalty — the Empress-Queen Victoria's offspring — showed up at the Palace, like the Grand Duchess George of Russia and Princess Victoria of Schleswig-Holstein. Two years and one month later their subjects began digging trenches across the continent and women, land girls and military auxillaries, began donning trousers for real, rather than as a stage act.

There have been nearly eighty such shows since, but the next one was not to be until the other side of the cataclysm, in 1919. And in one sense, the first was the last. As Raymond Mander and Joe Mitchenson wrote in their classic book *British Music Hall*, "the gods, jealous of whom they are said to love, decided themselves that the music hall was to die young. From the first named music hall of 1848 to 1912 is only a short span of sixty-four years and by the end of the next fifty years there would not be a working music hall as such left in London."

No more jokes

I'd like to see a Tank come down the stalls,
Lurching to ragtime tunes, or "Home, Sweet Home",
And there'd be no more jokes in Music-halls
To Mock the riddled corpses round Bapaume

BLIGHTERS BY SIEGFRIED SASSOON, FEBRUARY 4 1917:
WRITTEN ON LEAVE FROM THE WESTERN FRONT, AFTER A
VISIT TO THE MUSIC HALL.

Vesta Tilley doing her
bit, complete with
Kaiser Bill's helmet.

ONE SUNLIT AFTERNOON, early spring, I am in
Belgium, at Spanbroekmolen. This is on what was,
ninety years ago, the Western Front. In June 1917 the
British detonated a million pounds of explosives under the
German lines. So loud was the explosion that it could be
heard on the home front, in London. Spanbroekmolen now
is intensely green countryside and between a duck pond
and a barn is the Lone Tree cemetery. There I find
splendidly tended Irish graves. Most of these are of Royal Irish Rangers who
died on June 7, 1917. Maybe they died accidentally — strange concept —
when the British mines went up, or when the Germans replied with an
artillery barrage. I am near Ypres, where on the towering Menim gate is the
inscription: "To the armies of the British Empire who stood here from 1914
to 1918". They stood and, naturally, they fell, shot, blown up, gassed.

Forty years separated George W Hunt's 'Jingo Song' of 1877 and Sassoon's
Blighters; four decades, and that chasm between jingoism and realism, fantasy
redcoats and muddy khaki, dreams of glory and industrialised killing. But the
British army marched off in 1914 singing the hits of the music hall.

There was a contrast between those songs which went over well in the
British halls — echoing 'Jingo' — and those that suited the trenches. Not that
there isn't a literature of Tommies taking the night air at the Holborn Empire
and the Empire Leicester Square. And some songs crossed over everything. 'It's
A Long Way To Tipperary' was a music hall song written by Jack Judge, of
Birmingham, England. Judge's Tipperary contacts were two grandparents. No
matter, Tipperary was where the rainbow ends, Nirvana by way of Piccadilly
and Leicester Square and sung by the British, the Germans, the Russians —
and the Irish soldiers of the British Empire. It was first taken up, the story
goes, when a London *Daily Mail* reporter, in Boulogne, watched the arrival of
the British Army. He was much taken, apparently, by a smart battalion singing
'Tipperary'; the Connaught Rangers, they were — Irish soldiers.

You can all love me!

Jolly good luck to the girl who loves a soldier,
Girls, have you been there?
You know we military men
Always do our duty everywhere.
Jolly good luck to the girl who loves a soldier,
Really good boys are we.
Girls, if you'd like to love a soldier,
You can all love me!

FROM VESTA TILLEY'S 'JOLLY GOOD LUCK TO THE GIRL
WHO LOVES A SOLDIER', RECORDED IN JUNE 1915.

The 'Great Little Tilley', a very conservative path to success.

VESTA TILLEY, THE great actor Ellen Terry told the audience on the night of the star's farewell performance in 1919, "does not know what she has done for England. She made us laugh when, God knows, we needed to laugh."

But now most of England, and the United States, where she was also a huge draw, has forgotten the woman who dominated the music hall and vaudeville stage from the 1880s into — and through — the First World War. For the genius of Vesta Tilley, born Matilda Powles in Worcester in 1864, is now as remote as the Empire on which the sun never set and the blood never dried, and it is an art that has almost vanished from the stage.

With songs like 'At The Races', 'Burlington Bertie' ("He'll fight and he'll die like an Englishman") and 'Following In Father's Footsteps', Tilley, petite, proper and deeply patriotic, brought male impersonation to a level and subtlety never seen before, or since, on the British stage. She also left in her wake a certain smile, a hint of ambiguity, which is perhaps even more incomprehensible in a twenty-first century of literal-mindedness and quack psychology.

By the age of five, as "happy rogues and vagabonds" as she put it, Vesta was touring the country with her father. He was "Harry Ball the Tramp Musician" with his "wonderful performing dog" Fathead, she was "The Great Little Tilley", and having concluded that "female costume was rather a drag" she began male impersonation in 1872. Two years later she added the name Vesta, and gravitated to stardom — with a massive female following. In 1889 her father died, and in 1890 she married Walter de Frece, who with Edward Moss and Oswald Stoll were the entrepreneurs who dominated British music hall. Soon she was being greeted by Tony Pastor in New York as "England's greatest comedienne". It was an act which took in the *Royal Variety Performance* of 1912 — the then Queen averted her eyes to avoid seeing a woman's legs — and stayed on the road until 1919. De Frece became a knight and a Conservative MP, and the couple retired to Monte Carlo. On September 16 1952, seven months after the accession to the throne of Queen Elizabeth II, Lady de Frece, the woman who once sang 'May Queen Victoria Reign' ("Till ballet girls' clothes reach down to their toes") died, while visiting London.

Mystery of the East

I'll eat the way they do
With a pair of wooden sticks
And I'll have Ching Ling Foo
Doing all his magic tricks

FROM IRVING BERLIN'S
'FROM HERE TO SHANGHAI' (1917).

IT WAS THE early 1900s, and the older imperialisms, China and Russia, were beginning to implode. In the Far East the Japanese and Russian Empires were at war. By 1905 the latter was gripped by revolution, the modern world collided with the ancient. Mass stage entertainment in that late Imperial era could mean magic, make-believe, and — in that fleeting technological moment post-electricity, pre-Hollywood — illusion and illusionists.

Just after Christmas, 1904, a new play, about the boy who wouldn't grow up, opened at London's Duke of York's Theatre. Nina Boucicault flew as Peter Pan, with Gerald du Maurier as Mr Darling and Captain Hook, and Hilda Trevelyan as Wendy. JM Barrie's play, backed by the New York Empire's Charles Frohmann was, said *The Times* on December 28 1904, "a thing of pure delight... as delightful a fantasy of childhood as we ever remember seeing on stage".

In London in those early years of the twentieth century, the Hungarian-Jewish magician and illusionist Ehrich Weiss — the great Harry Houdini —having taken his adopted homeland, the United States, by storm conquered London's Alhambra and Hippodrome. In doing so he generated a host of imitators, who, to build their acts, went in search of the exotic, the alien — and the orientalist.

Assessing the surreal anachronism that was the Chinese Empire *The Times* reported, early in 1905, "aged reactionaries like the eunuch Li-lien Ying" were still the Empress-dowager's main advisers". China was a place to be carved up, it was a place of morbid fascination, mystery, saleable in movies, pulp fiction — Sax Rohmer's first Fu Manchu story was to appear eight years later —and on stage.

The same night that *Peter Pan* opened, and entered history, the Hippodrome in Leicester Square came up with a new variety bill. Its highlights were Mr Woodward's performing sea lions and seals, the "Butterflies In Fairieland" spectacular and "the Original Chinese Magician", forty-three-year-old Chung Ling Soo. The Chinaman was very well received, even if his finale, the "condemned to death trick" in which he caught bullets in mid-air, and dropped them on a plate, was dismissed by *The Times* as "too unreal to interest any person having the slightest familiarity with guns". Indeed the essence of the trick was that the bullet was never fired, since the gunpowder exploded below the barrel.

But the Hippodrome's star was not the sole Original Chinese Magician in town. At New Year 1905, across Leicester Square at the Empire, Ching Ling Foo opened, complete with his eleven-strong troupe of acrobats, singers and jugglers. These included his wife and diminutive daughter Chee Toy. Singing sentimental English ballads, Chee Toy brought the house down. She was irresistible, reported *The Times*, and "to watch the changing emotion on her little round face, with its bead-like eyes is a real delight". As for fifty-year-old Ching Ling Foo, once, apparently, one of the three magicians appointed to the court of Peking, well, there had been plenty of magicians who had produced a bowl of goldfish from underneath a handkerchief, but none who had

From the West Coast of California to the West End of London,
there was a time for Chung Ling Soo.

accomplished the trick while performing a double somersault.

That winter the two magicians traded insults and challenges across Leicester Square. But there was a catch. On stage Chung Ling Soo was a man of no words, offstage he would only speak through an interpreter. But that too was an illusion. Before Chung Ling Soo on the vaudeville boards in the United States, there had been a magician called Robinson, The Man

109

Of Mystery. And before that there had been Billy Robinson. When pressed, Chung Ling Soo claimed a Scottish father and Cantonese mother, but the reality of Chung Ling Soo was William Ellsworth Robinson, with two Scottish parents, and a birthplace not in China, but Brooklyn, New York City in 1861. Just as Houdini had plucked his stage name from the father of modern magicianship, Jean Eugene Robert-Houdin, so Chung Ling Soo had taken his name from — Ching Ling Foo.

Chung Ling Soo continued with his act, even if he was accused of offering to scab during the 1907 British music hall strike, and even if it was Ching Ling Foo who was featured in Irving Berlin's song. But by 1918 the American's career was waning, there were rumours of discord in Chung Ling Soo's marriage and by late March 1918, in London, he wasn't playing Leicester Square, but the unglamorous Wood Green Empire, in suburban north-east London. But the vogue for the mysterious east persisted. The hit West End musical of the time scrambled China and Ali Baba into Chu Chin Chow and even if Oswald Stoll's Wood Green Empire was unexotic, it was new, having opened six years earlier, and big, not as big as the Hackney Empire or the Coliseum, but, with 1,840 seats, one of the halls that marked the end of the golden age of variety theatre construction.

That Saturday night March 23, 1918, Chung Ling Soo was booked to play two houses at Wood Green. It was a desperate weekend in a Britain exhausted by almost four years of world war. Two days before, the German army had begun its last great push on the western front, sweeping back across France, shelling Paris, and unleashing artillery exchanges that could be heard — and were rattling windows — in Dover on the south coast of England.

The first house went without incident, then came the second house, and yet again, as it had been for twenty-five years, there was Chung Ling Soo's "condemned to death" trick. Witnesses were called from the audience to "verify" that there had been no deceit, and Olive, the magician's wife, picked up the twelve-year-old gun, and fired.

"My God," cried out Chung Ling Soo, aka Robinson, The Man Of Mystery. "Something has happened! Lower the curtain."

His wife rushed forward. The old gun had malfunctioned. The gunpowder had finally sent two bullets on their way. The following day, as the casualties of the Kaiser's final throw of the dice were piling up in France, at Wood Green Cottage Hospital, in north London, plain Billy Robinson of Brooklyn died of his injuries, leaving little but smoke and mirrors, raw material for a portfolio of conspiracy theories. Was it his wife? Was it his agent? Did they work together? His old rival, Ching Ling Foo, died four years later. And on October 31, 1926, the incomparable Houdini died in Detroit from peritonitis, triggered by a blow to the stomach received while demonstrating his strength.

The Wood Green Empire continued as a variety theatre until 1955, was transformed into an early commercial television studio. Later most of it was demolished, and replaced by a supermarket. Now all that remains of the place where an "unreal" routine of 1904 ended in tragedy fourteen years on, is a fragment of façade, and the enigma of Chung Ling Soo. But Peter Pan, of course, never died.

Big-boot dance

HE WAS A Kent farmer and innkeeper's sixteenth child; he was born with twelve slightly webbed fingers and took his name from Arthur Orton, the unsuccessful claimant in the 1871 Tichborne inheritance case. Orton was a big man; Harry Relph, "Little Tich", never grew beyond four feet six inches.

But Little Tich, who first appeared on stage in public houses as a ten-year-old in the late 1870s, and featured at one of the last pleasure gardens — in Gravesend — went on to become a towering music hall star in London, New York and Paris (and rather less successful in Australia), from the 1890s into the late 1920s. Highly intelligent, complex — and part of the backbone of the 1907 variety artists strike — such was his impact that in 1910, in the era of the entente cordiale, Tich, who had made himself fluent in French, was made an officier of the Academie Française.

Little Tich had soon abandoned a childhood blackface routine and focused on comedy and dancing. And at the centre of his dancing was

Little Tich and the amazing footwear: He was smaller than Queen Victoria, but unlike her got to join the Academie Francaise...

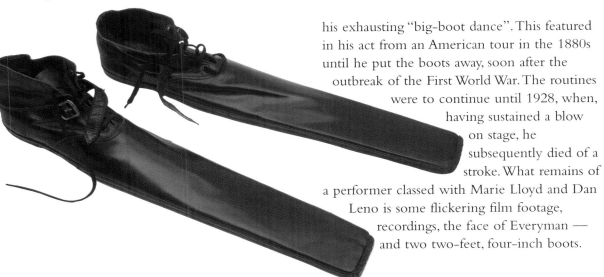

his exhausting "big-boot dance". This featured in his act from an American tour in the 1880s until he put the boots away, soon after the outbreak of the First World War. The routines were to continue until 1928, when, having sustained a blow on stage, he subsequently died of a stroke. What remains of a performer classed with Marie Lloyd and Dan Leno is some flickering film footage, recordings, the face of Everyman — and two two-feet, four-inch boots.

The meaning of America

The face of the Twentieth Century: Charlie Chaplin (*centre*) in 1895.

HIS WAS THE most famous face in the world. It registered determination, uncertainty, sympathy, impudence, humour — and that shock, experienced by millions of people around the planet, of their early encounters with the new and terrifying industrial order. His life began amidst the Alhambras and Empires of Victorian Britain; it was to encompass global media empires, conjured out of celluloid and wood pulp. It would end in the age of men on the moon.

The childhood of Charlie Chaplin was marked by destitution, rejection and madness. And on his way, as he wrote in his autobiography, his employment took in spells as a newsvendor, printer, toy-maker, glass blower and doctor's boy. But, most of all, his was a career moulded on the music hall stages of Edwardian Britain, at the Empires of Liverpool and Hackney and Streatham and Cardiff, the Tivolis, and the Alexandras and at times "alone in strange towns, alone in back rooms, rarely meeting anyone until the evening performance, only hearing my own voice when I talked to myself".

Charlie Chaplin was born on April 16 1889. His father was a music hall singer, and his mother — whose neglected talent Chaplin never ceased to extol — had been a *soubrette*, with a brief and unsuccessful time on the halls. He had an older brother, Sydney, and they had, Charlie wrote, "a brotherly love that has lasted throughout my life".

His father largely abandoned the family. He was to die at thirty-seven, an alcoholic. His mother, caught in a relentless spiral of poverty, fought to subsist by needlework but, by the time Charlie was six, had been confined, for the first time, in a lunatic asylum. She was to return to such institutions until her multi-millionaire son

relocated her to California in the wake of the First World War.

Then at the age of nine, Charlie joined the Eight Lancashire Lads — and thus in the last two years of the nineteenth century began his performing career with the touring music hall troupe. It would then be three years before he returned to the stage, mainly touring in a dramatisation of *Sherlock Holmes* — and falling in love with its American heroine, the future silent movie star Marie Doro.

Then, in 1908, via Sydney Chaplin, Charlie was introduced to Fred Karno. The impresario had turned the art of the comedy sketch into the creation of a production line, with Karno companies pumping their work into the variety houses not only of Britain, but of continental Europe — which took Chaplin to the Folies Bergere — and, crucially, to the United States.

What Karno was doing was anticipating the structure of mass entertainment in the twentieth century. What Chaplin was about to do was carry a spark of genius across the Atlantic and into the medium that would one day destroy the variety theatres.

In 1910 when Chaplin arrived for the first time in New York, and on Broadway, he wrote that "the meaning of America came to me" — and it was where he belonged. In 1912 he returned for a second tour. For him life on the stage ended one night in Kansas City. He had been made an offer by the Keystone Film Company in Los Angeles. The world had turned, and for him the world of the Empires had vanished forever.

Gaining altitude

That Nureyev's farewell British tour began in a Wearside variety theatre must say something, In the falling of the mighty there can be fewer greater losses of altitude... than from Covent Garden to the Sunderland Empire.
The Times

BY 1925 THE 63-year-old Sunderland architect T.R. Milburn could look back on a career during which, together with his brother William, he had designed some thirteen theatres, and worked on a further nine. He had collaborated with the great Frank Matcham, as at South Shields in the late 1890s, and in some cases — such as the Cardiff Empire in 1915 — obliterated the earlier Matcham theatre. But the pre-First World War variety boom was long gone. Cardiff had been the last complete theatre the Milburns had produced, and they were beginning to turn their attention towards cinemas.

It was in 1925 that Milburn visited the United States. And there he encountered the work of architect Thomas Lamb. Lamb was born in Dundee in 1870. His family had moved to New York while he was a child. By the turn of the century Lamb was working for the city's Bureau of Buildings. It was during that time that he encountered two men who were to revolutionise movie distribution and movie venues, William Fox and Marcus Loew. In 1908, with the Nicoland, on Westchester Avenue in the Bronx, Lamb created what is considered New York's first custom-made cinema.

Just as Matcham rode the variety boom to create Empires around Britain, so Lamb was the architect behind a chain of super-cinemas that were to span the Americas, and colonise Australia, Asia and Europe. And Lamb was just one figure. As it was in power politics, it was to be in show business, one empire superseded another, that of the United States, translating popular culture from penny dreadfuls, vaudeville and drama, into new style, celluloid, shellac and radio waves.

A key element in Lamb's work, which impressed Milburn, was the New Yorker's use of steel girders in theatre design to suspend large, wide-circle balconies. The result, in the absence of pillars, was a much-improved prospect of the stage, essential for movies, good for live shows. But who, in Britain, would want to build new variety theatres? Re-enter Moss Empires.

I drive into the spin of dual carriageways and roundabouts around Sunderland and consider insecurity. Sunderland lives in the shadow of larger, flashier Newcastle-upon-Tyne, a few miles up the A1. Sunderland's football team is overshadowed by that of Newcastle and Newcastle has Sting and Eric

Burdon and the Animals and Lindisfarne and Michael Caine in *Get Carter* and famous municipal crooks like T. Dan Smith in the 1960s and fog on the Tyne and the Bridge. Sunderland, I think, has a Nissan car works. If the citizens of Sunderland think of theatres, they can brood on Newcastle's magnificent Theatre Royal and the Royal Shakespeare Company based there, when in the north, and what is the Sunderland Empire famous for?

Stage acts complained about dying on stage in front of Wearside audiences who, it was said, lacked enthusiasm. Frank Thornton did not lack enthusiasm. In 1907, the Sunderland Empire was one of the jewels in his Northeast Circuit — which had become an ally of the mighty Moss Empires — and he had Vesta Tilley lay the foundation stone of the place. She was the big hit of its opening night, working through her Piccadilly Johnny, Soldier Tommy Atkins, and Eton Schoolboy routines I guess. Not that she mentioned it in her memoirs. And when the Empire faced closure in 1959, Stan Laurel from California, who had trod its boards in his youth wrote that he hadn't thought "it would last as long as it did".

But it survived. In 1959 Sunderland Council became the first authority in Britain to buy their local theatre. It continued under municipal control until the end of the twentieth century when the council leased it, in the end, to the vast American conglomerate, Clear Channel.

When the council had it, there was the Nureyev disaster when the dancer limped on stage with a bandaged ankle and triggered patronising articles about the northeast of England in the London press, and then there was the night in 1976 when the South African actor and comedian Sid James was performing in a farce called *The Mating Game*. Halfway through he did die, of a heart attack, on stage. People remember these things.

I get lost and, parking in an empty high-rise car park, contemplate the local pride and joy, the Stadium of Light, home of Sunderland football club. The Milburns, the Sunderland-born brothers, William and T.R. designed the Empire, over the road from the Dun Cow public house and the Sunderland Minster. A tower topped by a dome, but, outside, the place lacks charisma.

But then there is Sarah Clarke of the Empire. We go through the foyer, past pensioners queuing for the matinee. There are a lot of them and they are laughing and eating ice cream. We go into the auditorium and it is vast, with twin cupolas, baroque, unexpected, magnificent.

Dominic Stokes, the manager, says later that the design of the Sunderland Empire is wonderfully odd, different, a place the Milburns designed so that one audience could go in and another leave without them ever seeing one another. It was just a question of following the right routes. How did you get into theatre I ask him, what got you started? "It was when I was a child," he says. "My parents took me to see *Barnum* in the West End, in London, and

I thought it was superb and I still do."

Phineas T. Barnum goes on doing it, I think.

Sarah Clarke loves the Sunderland Empire I decide, and what I consider is the radiation coming off it. Born in nearby Washington, she first entered the Empire in the late 1980s, sat in the front row on free tickets. It was work experience; she did performing arts at university.

Get a proper job, her parents had said but then her father had seen her perform in a local drama group. "You have to do this," he said to her. "This is amazing."

We stare at the stage. "They come here all the time now," she says.

Sarah Clarke worked at the Empire when it was council-controlled. It was fine, musicals and one-night-stands, plays and tribute bands and stand-ups like Chubby Brown. It is curious I think, how local acts survive and no one notices in London, or New York or Toronto because if it ain't big city it is nowhere. Blue notes: in 1860, in the big city there was Renton Nicholson in the Coal Hole, in 1990 there was Chubby Brown at the Sunderland Empire.

The balance of the programmes has changed now, she says. Big musicals which never die in Sunderland because the audiences just lap them up. I think about the ironies. The variety theatres that survived the bombs of the 1940s, and television in the 1950s and demolition in the 1960s were saved by diligent local authorities and money from the arts council. Now these places exist as entertainment motorways, down them are driven the spectacles.

Why? I say. Why don't they just go to the pictures? The movies?

"Because theatre is magic. It is *there,* isn't it?" she says. "That's what people say, not just me. It is right in front of you and there are all these other people reacting to what is on that stage exactly when you are. There is that whole experience of being in that with somebody else. And when you go to the pictures that's bland isn't it? It isn't real. Here you may be sitting next to children crunching away, but it is really happening. People come to see *Starlight Express* and *Miss Saigon* and really stunned by it all, because it is so big."

The first big-scale show she saw at the Empire was *Cats* in 2003. It was the first time that she had ever seen the place packed out. We stare at the stage; a musician is finishing a run-though. "People," she goes on, "are in awe of what they are seeing and I was. *Starlight Express* was such a spectacle, so big, something audiences don't think can be done and Lloyd-Webber does it. You don't believe it."

The Empire gets a lot of ballet and opera, she goes on. Ellen Kent; the Birmingham Royal Ballet sells out traditional fairy tale ballets and people then go on to the more difficult stuff because they have seen the ballets.

They come back every time. "They trust the Empire, they trust what we are telling them and people in Sunderland have really reacted to it. God, it's about time!" Sarah Clarke says. "We have the Theatre Royal up the road and for years we have been the poor little sister and now we aren't and that is what people want. They now ask what's on at the Empire before they look at anything else."

"Clear Channel was the catalyst," she says. And I think about Lloyd-Webber and vast American conglomerates. "Clear Channel is why the Empire gets the shows," she goes on. "And once people just came from Sunderland but now, what with the motorways, people come from miles away. The one thing people in Sunderland are proud of is the football team. But now, and I wouldn't have said this a few years ago, this place, because of what's happened in it and how it has changed, how it has given people what they want to see. Well, their loyalty to the place as well, they are just proud of where they live. For so many years Sunderland has been compared to Newcastle as this bright shining star and Sunderland — well it's not like that any more."

The Sunderland Empire, inside and out.

I wouldn't have missed this for the world

THEY WENT WITH the territory, the profusion of Imperials and Empires in late nineteenth and early twentieth century Canada. There was the Imperial Opera House in Vancouver in 1889 — opera houses were a useful nineteenth-century yardstick for the expansion of western culture — an Empire Theatre in Montreal in the 1890s, and Edmonton managed three Empires between 1906 and 1920, while Saskatoon built one in 1910. And then there were Keith-Albee organisation's two almost identical Imperials, one in Saint John, New Brunswick, and one, now the Centre Cinéma Impérial, in Montreal.

The Albee-Keith policy was simple. Get local money working, in this case through the Saint John Amusements Company. A renowned Philadelphia architect, Albert E. Westover was brought in and, five months after its Montreal sister, on September 13, 1913, the Imperial opened as a vaudeville roadhouse. It was on the edge of Uptown, on King's Square — he being George III — and round the corner from Canada's steepest main street. It opened when the town, seventy-five miles from the border with the United States, over the Bay of Fundy from Nova Scotia, already had another six theatres.

But it is the Imperial, Canada's most beautiful theatre according to the Toronto Star, which has survived. In 1929, post *The Jazz Singer*, it became the Capitol cinema, and stayed that way until 1957, when it was taken over by a church. Then, in 1982 a local woman, Susan Bate, and a taxi driver, Jack MacDougal, put down a dollar as a down-payment to raise a million and buy the Imperial for the town. There was no professional arena, says the Imperial's general manager Peter Smith. People were using the local high school for meetings. MacDougal and Bate raised the money, and Can.$11.4 million and twelve years later the Imperial was back in business.

People in Saint John, Smith goes on, ask two questions of visitors. "Where are you from?" — which means where were you born? and "What do you think of St John?" People here, says Smith, in their strange, reserved, weird, introverted, don't-want-to-shout-about-it Canadian way are absolutely proud of their Imperial. Cleo Laine came here to perform and stood on that wonderful stage in the afternoon for the sound check and said "forget it, no need, the acoustics are fantastic".

They are, says Smith. "There is something special about this place. Look, I have worked as a producer around Canada but it is the geometry of the Imperial. A show is coming up, and you stand there on stage and it is as if the auditorium is there to embrace you."

Back in 1913 B.F. Keith's son and heir promised a hands-off policy, but suggested the theatre should keep an eye open for the good acts coming its way. Amongst them, in that era of magic, was Harry Houdini. In town, says

Smith, and visiting the local lunatic asylum he was shown a straitjacket — and got an idea for an act. The tours are different now, he says.

But the Imperial is still a presenting theatre and a roadhouse. "Most shows come here for one night. We do literally everything, classical music, straight music, circus, opera, stand-up comedians, Broadway material, a drama festival, a dance festival. There is ballet, neo-classical, flamenco, belly dancing, clog dancing; the Royal Winnipeg pulls in a crowd. What do you want? Opera, classical, hip-hop, rock, the Symphony New Brunswick, Opera New Brunswick, *Tosca* — scaled down, *The Mikado*. Two local companies do plays, one is amateur, they tend to do the more challenging stuff, *Oleanna* the other month, Shakespeare, and there is a professional company. We work at least 185 days a year. In the summer we get little activity —"

"Why?" I ask. "People have boats," he says, "other things, tents, the great outdoors. "People say that Saint John is a blue-collar town, sure it is blue-collar, but there are a lot of wealthy people, a lot of hi-tech industry."

There is uncertainty about money, says Smith but there is, always is, and these days it is harder to get people's attention. People are less willing to commit themselves as to just what they are going to be doing on the 15th. But sometimes they do, and it works." You know, one evening I am standing there and a guy comes out and says to me that he was given tickets. And then he says, 'I wouldn't have missed this for the world'."

The Imperial (*above*) in St. John, Canada's most beautiful theatre? And (*below left opposite*) an early visitor, inspecting the local straitjackets, was Harry Houdini...

119

The same marble

A new theatre owned by Moss Empires Limited was opened at Southampton on Saturday evening when the new musical play Winona *was presented by Mr Russell James in association with Madame Olga Treskoff. The theatre has seating accommodation for over 2000 persons and has a roof garden. The stage is one of the largest in the country, its width being 80ft with a depth of 60ft and it can be illuminated to the extent of 100,000 candle power.*

THE TIMES, MONDAY DECEMBER 24, 1928.

SOMETIME AFTER NEW YEAR, 2005, I am sitting in a modern, anonymous office next door to Southampton's Mayflower. The theatre's Paul Lewis is speculating as to why, three quarters of a century earlier, Moss Empires launched their last, doomed, theatre expansion.

That last Moss hurrah did yield contracts for the Milburns. There was the Liverpool Empire in 1925, the Edinburgh Empire in 1928 — where once again the brothers superseded an earlier Matcham theatre — and the Dominion in London in 1929. In 1931 they rebuilt another Matcham, the Glasgow Empire.

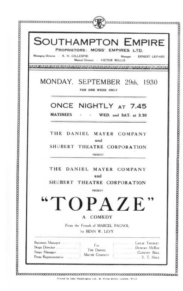

That was the variety house where, a couple of decades later, the young comedian Des O'Connor fainted on stage; the theatre where, after the comedian Mike Winters had endured fifteen minutes of barracking and stony silence, he was joined on stage by his brother, Bernie. "Good God," came a cry from the back of the stalls, "there's two of them...". The Glaswegians generally welcomed Americans, but it was the theatre where, said English entertainers, if they liked you, they let you live; it was a theatre which, in 1963, got demolished, like, sadly, most of the Milburns' work.

But not the Southampton Empire of my own childhood. Until 1987 the Mayflower was the Gaumont. But until 1950 the Gaumont was the Southampton Empire.

"Look," says Paul Lewis, "Moss Empires came to a south coast town, Southampton, and thought 'we have everything going for ourselves here, we are on to a winner'. So they build this massive theatre. They still have the idea that theatre is the big thing. There is not much wireless — radio was more 1930s — cinema was still silent, and it was just before the great depression."

We agree it was bad timing. There was *The Jazz Singer* and then there was the Wall Street crash. On that latter day the famous Jack Hylton Band was topping the bill at the last great central London music hall, the Holborn Empire. Hylton sold a lot of 78rpm shellac and would have pulled in a crowd. But crash equals slump equals war equals Blitz. The glorious Holborn Empire was bombed in 1941 and finally demolished in 1960. The Leicester Square Empire was advertising dancers on that day in 1929, just like in the 1890s when they outraged Mrs Ormiston Chant. But by 1929 they were on celluloid, in the *Hollywood Revue* with twenty-five all-talking-singing and dancing world famous stars and a chorus of two hundred. How could *Winona*, at the Southampton Empire, compete with that?

EMPIRE THEATRE. SOUTHAMPTON

Now it flourishes as the Mayflower; then, from the 1920s into the 1950s, it fought a losing battle as the Empire Southampton...

They ran live performances at the Southampton Empire for the first five years, says Paul Lewis. "The names, the acts, the plays are amazing. Gracie Fields, Anna Pavlova, Paul Robeson..." He reads from playbills: "*White Cargo* 'a vivid play of primitive unvarnished life in the tropics', the 'world famous Pavlova', *Lilac Time, Cavalleria Rusticana, I Pagliacci, Topaze, Rio Rita, Jew Suss, Faust, Madame Butterfly*."

I examine a poster. Carl Brisson with Helen Gilliland and George Graves in "Franz Lehar's masterpiece *The Merry Widow*".

The Jazz Singer, in which Mr Al Jolson may be both seen and heard is only in part a "talking" film. Most of the story is told with the assistance of "captions" but we hear half a dozen of the songs for which Mr. Jolson is justly renowned on both sides of the Atlantic, and also one or two fragments of conversation. These appear as interruptions in the flow of visual images, and effectually encompass the ruin of the story, but they are most interesting as the most considerable attempt to break the silence of the film drama which has yet been witnessed in this country...
Synchronization has been almost perfectly achieved.

FROM *THE TIMES*'S REVIEW OF *THE JAZZ SINGER*, AT THE PICCADILLY THEATRE LONDON, SEPTEMBER 28, 1928.

It was a long-running act: Ethel Merman as Annie Oakley, in 1946, showing off to ersatz cowpoke pal, actor Ray Middleton, the Winchester rifle the real Annie used in her 1887 European tour.

"These are the biggest names of the time, and they were in Southampton," says Paul Lewis. And the audiences weren't showing up, I say. Not there, and less so everywhere.

"Not in the numbers they were expecting. And in 1933 they went over to showing films. There were occasional evenings of live entertainment, a main film and some variety acts. The Empire was built close to Southampton railway station so they could have a siding for touring shows to pull in and be shifted off the track. But during the Second World War it was almost entirely films, because there weren't the touring shows. And in the years after the war, there was no live entertainment. But then in September 1950, they got *Annie Get Your Gun*."

Yes, I say, I remember *Annie Get Your Gun*.

In mid-1940s New York the lyricist Dorothy Fields, daughter of Lew Fields, of the comic duo Weber and Fields of the Weber and Fields Music Hall, late Imperial Music Hall on Broadway, decided that Ethel Merman would make a great Annie Oakley. The plan was a musical about the sharp-shooter-cum-wild west star. Fields collaborated with her brother Herbert on the book and Irving Berlin, noting, critically, the wild success of the cornpone *Oklahoma!* provided words and music.

Wall Street Panic Record Selling Of Stocks Heavy Fall In Prices: A Niagara of liquidation fell on the American Stock Exchange today. For three hours trading was completely demoralized with blocks of 10,000, 15,000 and 20,000 shares of stock pressing for sale and prices melting away five and ten points at a time. Never before even at the outbreak of the Great War, was there such a volume of transactions.

THE TIMES REPORTS "BLACK THURSDAY" OCTOBER 24 1929, THE BEGINNING OF THE WALL STREET CRASH.

There was 'You Can't Get A Man With A Gun' and 'The Girl That I Marry' and 'Anything You Can Do (I Can Do Better)' and 'There's No Business Like Show Business'. It opened in 1946 and ran for 1147 performances at the Imperial Theatre on Broadway. It had an even longer run in a London grey, austere and bombed. By the time it toured to grey, austere, bombed Southampton, one Peggy Powell had replaced Merman.

"There were queues round the theatre," says Paul Lewis. "They only used to do booking ten days in advance, nowadays we book a year in advance. And not many people had phones in 1950. They took so much cash that they couldn't get it into the safe, so they put it in mailbags and took it up to the Civic Centre police station and it was kept in cells overnight."

But *Annie* moved on. The movies came back, the Empire became the Gaumont, the variety shows dwindled, rock shows came in the 1960s, made money and went off to stadiums, arenas and muddy fields. The Empire/Gaumont owner, by then Rank Organisation, fresh from its role in turning off the British film industry's life support system, applied to turn it into a bingo hall, or a hole in the ground, or something. But this was decades on from the great 1950s and 1960s cull of variety theatres. In 1984 Southampton council purchased the theatre and after a £3 million refurbishment — funded by the local authority and the Arts Council — the theatre was handed over to a trust and rechristened the Mayflower. Southampton has a thing about the Mayflower. It remains collectively irritated that the Pilgrim Fathers, setting out from Southampton for America then sneaked, en route, into Plymouth, thus ensuring that the Devon seaport hogged the subsequent credit, brethren and publicity.

"The vision in 1928," says Paul Lewis, "was a big theatre and it didn't work. Well, suddenly it works. People can afford to go to the theatre and we are well-placed in terms of railways and motorways."

I look at a 1930s photograph of an Empire queue for *Snow White*. No cars, open-neck shirts, cloche hats, bonnets, prams; no sign of real poverty — these were people paying money to be entertained — but no real money either.

"It works because of the shows," he says. "When the Arts Council helped refurbishment to establish a circuit for opera and ballet they created a circuit for commercial musical product. There had been these really second-rate touring productions going round and there was the time when musicals seemed to be dead. What was there in the early 1970s? *Hair*?" He laughs. "It is the spectacle, any show that combines music and drama has a head start — as opera does in its own way."

As opera has since Gounod's *Faust* at the Canterbury in the 1850s and Caruso in New York in the 1890s.

The stuff of the 1920s stage, from Southampton to the West End: Stanley Holloway in The Co-Optimists pierrot show.

In the Thirties: with variety on the slide, the rise of the mighty Walt Disney organisation — *Snow White* and the Southampton queues...

We walk into the theatre. The Milburns did good work. Wonderful lurid green, turquoise, off-pink boxes, musicians rehearsing under art deco lights, Moorish embellishments, I catch Disraeli fleetingly taking a bow by the synthesiser. Up in the Gods, half a century on from my last visit, I can hear the conversation on stage and I wonder if I will drop off the edge of the world. On Seat E14 there is a dedication. "George", it says. "Fond memory brings the light of other days around me. Leslye." Theatres are magic, I think, again. Half a century ago I had thought I was looking at an up-to-date grown-up world. Now I realise it was the Milburns' 1920s world, persisting.

We descend into the foyer, the Milburn's grand stone staircase under our feet. "This particular kind of marble," says Paul Lewis, "comes from North Africa, or southern Spain. I was in Pompeii a few years ago and in the amphitheatre I looked down at the ground. There it was, the same marble."

The lapse of time

*During the course of this act the curtain will be lowered for a few seconds
to indicate the lapse of time.*

FROM THE PROGRAMME FOR ANTHONY KIMMINS'S *WHILE PARENTS SLEEP*, THE
EMPIRE THEATRE CLEETHORPES, WEEK COMMENCING NOVEMBER 25, 1946.

LITTLE EMPIRES LIVED off the late Victorian-Edwardian-Teddy Roosevelt
glow. Some withered when it flickered and died. Who now remembers
the Empire, Southport? Date of birth uncertain, but on December 3, 1909, a
venue for Winston Churchill, no longer the young Empire Leicester Square
protester, but a member of the radical Liberal British government, and billed
to orate. But Churchill had not allowed for the tide of history, in the shape
of Dora Marsden.

Soon to be the editor of the *Freewoman*, a paper demanding the vote and
equal rights for women, Dora descended from the heights of the Empire,
together with a band of her sisters, to confront Churchill, an opponent of
votes for women. Votes for women arrived in 1918, parity in voting in 1928,
but fate was less kind to the Empire Southport. It was demolished five years
later. The early 1930s were a terrible time for variety in Britain — and in
that Lancashire town in particular. It lost three theatres in two years.

The Empire, Newark New Jersey, born 1912 as a variety house, was a
tougher act. Post-First-World-War it survived on a diet of touring comics,
bump and grind, and strippers. Indeed it fleetingly boomed pre-Pearl
Harbor, after New York Mayor Fiorella LaGuardia's 42nd Street clean-up
campaign boosted Newark burlesque. But, in the cold-war 1950s, the Empire
itself got cleaned up. Closed in 1957, it was demolished in 1958.

When that glow went, some places survived, walked-past, unnoticed,
forgotten. Heading for Shirebrook, Derbyshire, I get lost around Chesterfield
and drive, swearing, on into the night. But there in Shirebrook is an Empire,
on a ridge, overlooking the town. A notice signalling into darkness says
"Leading To Thickley Bank". Back in 1910, when it opened, the Empire was
live acts and movies. In the end, I suppose, it was bingo.

The Empire, Shirebook, just off Station Road, smacks of an Edwardian
fire-station, dark red brick, arched, "Empire" etched into the stone, and there
is a worrying, fallen-down, "For Sale" sign. I knock on a door in an adjacent
terrace, an Alsatian barks. I back off. No, says the youth next door, staring at
the mad person out of the winter gloom and chill. He knows nothing about
it, an old building, right? Just an old building; back on to Station Road a bus
passes, "Ibiza, £39 from Doncaster", is pasted on its side.

Sometimes, post-glow, across a century, comes metamorphosis. On the outskirts of Birmingham, England, in St Paul's Road, I am greeted by Mr Gill at the entrance to the once Smethwick Empire. He is courteous, thoughtful, and bemused, I think, by my visit. The Empire's frontage is intact, a deft, elegant Edwardian mixture of arches and angles, built by a local architect, the same year as Shirebrook, but with its stage enlarged and dressing rooms extended in 1919. It survived fitfully until, in 1930, film took over its programme. It survived as a cinema at least until 1957. Externally, it still hints at a mid-twentieth century, second or third run movie house: *The Third Man* playing ten years on; *The Robe* back by popular demand; this week only, *Nudist Paradise*... Later the building became a banqueting hall.

"You will need a hat", says Mr Gill. His companion provides me with a blue scarf. I drape it sheepishly on my head, *Crimson Pirate*-style. "When we go in" explains Mr Gill, "you will need to genuflect."

In the communal area, once the foyer, tables are heaped with Indian vegetarian food. "Sunday is the main day for services," says Mr Gill. "But it is a most important thing that free food is here, every day, for everyone. There are a lot of very poor people."

In 1992 the local Sikh community took over the Empire and turned it into a gurdwara, a temple. Mr Gill lives in Derby, and works on Sikh welfare programmes.

We enter the temple, the old Empire's auditorium. I genuflect; Mr Gill explains that I should eat a small quantity of the dough a lady is kneading. She smiles at me. It is a Sikh host, I think, slightly sweet. The gurdwara is decorated with blue and orange pennants. Where once there was a stage, there is now a glittering golden shrine containing the *Guru Granth Sahib* holy book of the Sikhs. Taped music fills the hall, worshippers cluster in small groups on the carpeted floor. Above, the old music hall balcony is still in place; I catch Edwardian faces staring down, ripples of ancient applause.

"It was a good building and a good hall and we decided to make this a temple," says Mr Gill. Great, I say, once people came here purely for escape, now they come here for God as well. And they get a free meal too, I think. There is no money around, but there is heart in a heartless world. The Empire is alive. "A Sikh should make a visit once in the morning and once in the evening," says Mr Gill. Do you like it here, I ask. Yes, says Mr Gill. He likes it here. The English are honest, and that is a wonderful thing.

The trouble with Richmonders, says actor Gordon Bass, tour company director of Theatre IV, is that they are not natural, instinctive theatregoers. Theatre IV is a company focused on young people, that plays, he says, across the United States, east of the Mississippi, but its base is in Virginia at the Empire Theatre.

The Empire opened in downtown Richmond on Christmas night in 1911, went through changes, turned into a cinema and fell empty. "This place is gorgeous, right? Just gorgeous," says Bass. "It was a vaudeville house once, we took it over in 1987, and children are just wowed by it, it is such a grand space, beautiful to use, wonderful acoustics. And there is the whole thing about the magic of live performance. Last Christmas we did *A Christmas Carol*, I am the ghost of Jacob Marley, clanking, coming out of the trap in the floor. Did it work? I had kids peeing in their pants."

In Blackburn Lancashire, on a sunny morning, half a mile away from Ewood Park, another vast new football stadium, and home to Blackburn FC, businessman Malcolm Berry of the Thwaites Empire Theatre is talking about the world into which, in 1911, the new Cinematograph Hall, Ewood, the Empire Electric Theatre was born. "Clogs and shawls and mills," says Mr Berry, "dozens of cotton mills. The owners earned £1000 a week and the workers sixpence if they were lucky."

We pause. "I had a staff of 50 in my business," he goes on, "and I thought it was overcrowded sometimes. But then, well, we are talking nine hundred people in those mills."

And now they have all gone, I say. I drove over that historic industrial landscape that morning and they have all gone, all the mills. Even when I was here in the 1960s there were some left.

"When that theatre was built," he says, "it sat six hundred people downstairs. Six hundred people. It was tuppence at the front, fourpence at the back and sixpence in the gallery."

The locals didn't call it the Empire Electric Theatre. They called it the Barn. Like Shirebrook, it was a cine-variety. Sound effects were provided during the silent movie era, sandpaper, thunder-sheet, coconuts, a motor-horn. There were variety turns in the interval, a clog dancer performing on a plate, and baritone Jimmy Ainsworth who wrote, and performed songs, 'The Whitehaven Pit Disaster' and, 'The Ribble Valley'. The Electric's management, like, albeit on a more modest scale, Tony Pastor in New York, sold Ainsworth's songs for sixpence a go. The folk art of industrial Britain, rubbing up against the Keystone Cops and Charlie Chaplin in faraway California.

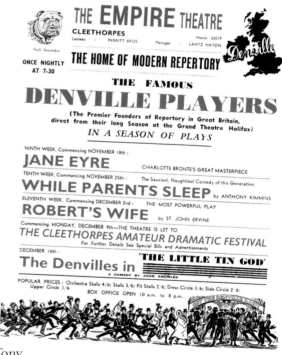

THE **EMPIRE** THEATRE
CLEETHORPES   Phone 62019
Lessees ·   PERRITT BROS.   Manager ·   LANTZ HAYDN

Nulli Secundus

ONCE NIGHTLY   **THE HOME OF MODERN REPERTORY**
AT 7-30

Denville

THE FAMOUS
DENVILLE PLAYERS
(The Premier Founders of Repertory in Great Britain, direct from their long Season at the Grand Theatre Halifax)
IN A SEASON OF PLAYS

NINTH WEEK, Commencing NOVEMBER 18th :
JANE EYRE   CHARLOTTE BRONTE'S GREAT MASTERPIECE
TENTH WEEK, Commencing NOVEMBER 25th :   The Sauciest, Naughtiest Comedy of this Generation
WHILE PARENTS SLEEP   by ANTHONY KIMMINS
ELEVENTH WEEK, Commencing DECEMBER 2nd :   THE MOST POWERFUL PLAY
ROBERT'S WIFE   by ST. JOHN ERVINE
Commencing MONDAY, DECEMBER 9th—THE THEATRE IS LET TO
THE CLEETHORPES AMATEUR DRAMATIC FESTIVAL
For Further Details See Special Bills and Advertisements
DECEMBER 16th :
The Denvilles in   "THE LITTLE TIN GOD"
A COMEDY BY JOHN KNOWLES

POPULAR PRICES : Orchestra Stalls 4/6; Stalls 3/6; Pit Stalls 2/6; Dress Circle 3/6; Side Circle 2 6;
Upper Circle 1/6   BOX OFFICE OPEN 10 a.m. to 8 p.m.

By 1974 the cinema had effectively closed. There were a couple of spells as a movie house for Blackburn's then new Asian community, but in 1979 the Blackburn Theatre Trust, comprising committed locals, purchased the one-time Barn for £12,000. "The old trust," says Mr Berry, "kept the roof on the building and gave us a platform to resurrect it. The success we have had is because of volunteers." Now it is a splendid, pretty little theatre.

"There wasn't a suitable building in Blackburn for local amateur theatre companies," says Mr Berry. "The aim was to provide a facility, for greater appreciation of the arts, in all forms, to be enjoyed by the citizens of Blackburn."

There were some rows, about direction, organisation. Some people quit. "I am not a theatre man. I am a businessman and chairman of the Gilbert and Sullivan Society," says Mr Berry. "Five people resigned from the theatre on one night."

The Lottery Fund provided £100,000 for a feasibility study, but no Lottery funding followed. The place didn't meet the specification. "We got pledges from companies," Mr Berry continues. "They would say, 'Do you mean that derelict cinema at Ewood?' But they coughed up, and the *Blackburn Telegraph* said they would back us.

"What I said is we need bums on seats. So we charged people £25 to be a bum and at our launch meeting people were coming up on stage, saying they would have ten seats."

The Thwaites Empire Theatre — Mr Berry got sponsorship from a local brewery — opened in October 2002. "Companies said yes to helping us because I was giving them some value, and they could put their literature into the theatre," says Mr Berry. His young, enthusiastic assistant, Ian Helm, takes me round. "When I hang my boots up," says Mr Berry as we walk out of the door, "Ian will take over."

The 1906 edition of the upmarket *Murray's Guide* described Cleethorpes as the "most crowded watering place in Lincolnshire". Because of "its easy access by railway," the *Guide* continued, "Cleethorpes is invaded daily during the summer by enormous crowds of excursionists from Yorkshire, Lancashire and the Midland counties".

Rain sweeps across the flat country around Grimsby. Cleethorpes is encircled by that industrial fishing port. Fishing is in decline, the crowded watering place is almost deserted on that late winter morning, the North Sea horizon is smudged into the rain and I struggle off the front, figuring out a location for the Cleethorpes Empire. The eight-hundred seat theatre went up, to delight non-*Murray*-reading excursionists, sometime in the 1890s. On Alexandra Road, neon flashes out of the mauled facade of a one-storey 1890s building. I thread around quacking one-arm bandits, teenage girls practising on dance step machines, teenage boys on Indie Five Hundred race machines. I pick out the manager.

His office is cramped and once, maybe, a dressing room. I am pessimistic, I ask John Lonsdale about the Empire. Hang on, he says and reaches into a desk drawer.

I had focused on the 1890s but these cuttings are the Cleethorpes Empire caught in winter 1946, that time of war crimes trials, shortages, industrial working parties, occupied zones, Communist takeovers and no TV sets. There are cuttings for Charles Denville's "celebrated Denville Stock Company in a season of the latest and greatest plays" plus "the Empire Theatre Orchestra under the direction of Tommy Hopkin". On offer is *Jane Eyre, Smilin' Through, Robert's Wife*, the "sauciest, naughtiest comedy of this generation", *While Parents Sleep*, and for "seasonal entertainment" *Rookery Nook*. Illness prevented Miss Sheila Bacon from her final performance in Terence Rattigan's *Flare Path*, so the *Grimsby News's* bouquet was received on her behalf by Miss Edna Dore, she, half a century on, of Mike Leigh, *Nil By Mouth* and *EastEnders*. Great, isn't it? says Mr Lonsdale. Yes, I say, great. One of the playbills depicts top-hatted swells flocking to the Empire, cramming in under the "Get The Denville Habit" arch, Piccadilly Johnnies in amber, trapped in the chill of austerity Britain, austerity Cleethorpes.

"This," says Mr Lonsdale, "is the stage." We are standing among the Super Jackpot and Rampage machines and on the stage itself there are pool tables. But Mr Lonsdale can trace the pattern of the Empire that was. There is no proscenium, I say.

"Come with me," he says. We move out of the auditorium-cum-arcade to the Victorian staircase. The upstairs floor is crammed with the detritus of the arcade's Laser game. "Look there," he says. At the end, in the darkness, is the proscenium arch of the 1890s. Under it, once, there was opera, seaside shows and the Denville players in *Night Must Fall*, during which, as reviewer "F.C.S." of the *Grimsby News* pointed out, "You can almost feel the chill of the descending night".

"It was bingo in the late 1970s and early 1980s," says Mr Lonsdale. "One day the Philistines came along and trashed the place, Victorian bay windows and all." We stumble, in the dark, with the whooping of electronics below, to the front of the building. Look here, he says, pointing out wood panelling over window frames. "Behind this," he says, "are the original stained glass windows. Great, isn't it?" Yes, I say, great.

The weather cleared. It seemed inevitable after Mr Lonsdale. I went off and ate haddock and chips at Ernie Becket's Fish Restaurant, voted best in the Grimsby area. There were kids being led on donkeys along that sunlit beach. "The best thing about Cleethorpes," Mr Lonsdale had said, "is that it is easy to get to."

That piano wire voice

Climbing the range
your ears pop like champagne
and your heart distends
with something other than relief

You can smell the peace up here.
The proportion, the narrowness.
Traitor, traitor whines that piano wire voice
as you swing past the Welcome sign

To find nothing is changed.
Overhead the clouds boil past,
low, friendly, meaning no harm

FROM *PROVINCIAL CITY*, BY BRUCE DAWE, POET, AND SOMETIME TEACHER IN TOOWOOMBA, QUEENSLAND, NORTH-EASTERN AUSTRALIA.

"TWO HOURS DRIVE from Brisbane," says the Toowoomba Empire's Andrew Mason. "This place," he goes on, "is the link between Brisbane, on the coast, and the Great Dividing Range. It is fertile land round here. It was a settlement on the way west, a health retreat"

Or, as it has been called, a hill station, near the crest of the Range, like Simla in the Punjab, and built around the same time. But Simla was where the British went to escape the summer heat of Delhi, Toowoomba, one hundred and fifty years ago, was a spot on the wagon route from Brisbane, ideal for servicing the farms of Darling Downs. The settlers called it the Swamp, which is what the Aborigines — who were driven out by the 1850s — were calling it with their Toowoomba, which meant either just swamp or "the native melon (toowoom) which grew by the swamp".

Toowoomba, second biggest inland city in Australia, voted (twice) the most liveable city in Australia, birthplace, in 1896, of the Lamington cake (sponge, coated in chocolate, rolled in desiccated coconut) named in honour of Lord Lamington, Tory Governor of Queensland, who, passing by, had wanted a snowball cake for tea. There was no cream around and so that afternoon he got the Lamington invented instead, now a national treasure. Toowoomba, a city of just under ninety thousand souls. "There are about

EMPIRE THEATRE, NEIL STREET, TOOWOOMBA, Q.

one hundred and fifty thousand people in the entire area," says Andrew Mason, "the shires push up against the city boundary."

In the 1990s a debate started about a cultural centre for Toowoomba. "The discussion split three ways," says Andrew Mason. "There were those who wanted a new facility, those who were opposed to any council spending on anything much, beyond roads and sewers, and those who wanted to renovate the Empire. It came down to a deciding vote on the council."

The Empire had been effectively derelict for more than two decades. "Rebuilding," says Andrew Mason, "was an amazing undertaking, it cost thirteen million Australian dollars. There were still people saying it was 'too big, they will never fill it'. But the town can grow into it. It seats 1,567, less now than it did all those years ago when it first opened."

That was the 1900s, and the days in Toowoomba of George Essex Evans. A barrister's son, Evans was born near Regent's Park, London. Educated in Wales and Jersey, Evans's father died when he was young, deafness ruled out the army, so the story of Evans became one more yarn of Empire, off to a new land to make a go of it. He arrived in Allora, Darling Downs with his brother and two sisters as an eighteen-year-old in 1881 and they took over a farm. But Evans was injured in a riding accident, and via some jobbing

Toowoomba and its Empire, in the days of the talkies.

journalism, a surveying expedition towards the wild Gulf Country of the north, more farming, a spell as a bailiff and some clerking, he ended up as Toowoomba's district registrar, married a widow with two children and supplemented his income with journalism and running a dairy and milk delivery. But it was Evans's poetry which turned him into a major figure in Queensland, and indeed in a young Australia — Prime Minister Alfred Deakin called him the country's national poet — as it moved to become, in 1901, a Commonwealth within the Empire:

> *In the slab-built, zinc-roofed homestead of some lately-taken run,*
> *In the tent beside the bankment of a railway just begun,*
> *In the huts of new selections, in the camps of man's unrest,*
> *On the frontiers of the nation, live the Women of the West*

Apart from *The Women Of The West*, he managed a poem, *Toowoomba*, on the "fair city", "the Mountain Queen" and its

> *Low wooded billows and steep summits hoary,*
> *Ridge, slope, and mountain crest*

which might have done something to offset that patronising English Fabian Beatrice Webb's comment from 1898 about the area's "sickly beauty".

Evans also set up the Austral arts festival, which put Toowoomba on the regional cultural map. "They got ten thousand people to it," says Andrew Mason. "There were a lot of arts groups, the Ladies Literary Society, the Toowoomba Philharmonic Society, and they are both still going." Evans even had the old jail turned into a hall, and it was from its stage, during the Austral festival, that his death, following a lethal, if unromantic, gallstones operation in Toowoomba, was announced in 1909.

Out of that post-Commonwealth cultural flurry emerged, two years later on June 29, 1911 the Empire, Toowoomba, and thus a 2,000 capacity meeting place — and movie house. In February 1933 the Empire was destroyed in the biggest fire in the history of the town, but the theatre was up and open again nine months later. Closed in the early 1970s, reborn in the 1990s, it reopened in June 1997.

"Then everyone has started raving about the place," says Andrew Mason, "The city is behind it, people are proud of it, they come, they bring their friends. I grew up in this town, my secret dream was always to work here. I'm thirty-four, the Empire was closed during much of my lifetime, but it is a fantastic old building and it is in the centre of the town. A lot of our older volunteers, the Friends of the Empire, they grew up going to the movies at

the Empire, they went courting at the theatre. People care about it, they work as ushers. They put out freshly cut flowers. They bake biscuits."

Most of the acts are pro, says Andrew Mason. Kris Kristofferson was through, so was Clive James with a chap playing a guitar and the Soweto Gospel Choir. "The Australian Chamber Orchestra got seven hundred people, which isn't bad," he says, "it isn't bad at all." Musicals go down well; the Empire put on its own *Chicago*, pulling in local talent, and *Grease* too. The Philharmonic Society and the Choral Society also put on musicals.

The actor Geoffrey Rush is the patron of the Empire Theatres Foundation. He is from Toowoomba; here, as a kid, he first encountered theatre. There is a youth programme, says Andrew Mason, young people get to do things in the theatre, and, every August there is the Shoot Out Toowoomba Film Making Festival where entrants, fifty-seven last time round, with around eight people per team, make a complete movie on VHS in twenty-four hours. Last time round the winners used the prize money to reshoot the film in Brisbane and then they won a best short film award with it, across the Pacific, in Santa Monica.

"Sometimes," says Andrew Mason, "kids come in, run around. And the parents say 'stop, sit down'. That saddens me. Kids should be excited. It is a theatre, after all, and a place with art deco style.

"Look," he goes on, "a lot of theatres in Queensland, newer places, are just brick boxes. People walk in here, and they feel the magic, a sense of occasion, community."

133

My name is Ticklebottom

Stan: I'm not the patient. He's the one who's insanitary.
Ollie: How dare you make such a statement! Why, I've never seen you before in my life... My name is Ticklebottom.
Doctor Berserk: Then what are you doing here?
Ollie: I came to see a relative and got in this room by mistake.

FROM *BIRDS OF A FEATHER*, THE LAST SKETCH EVER PERFORMED BY STAN LAUREL AND OLIVER HARDY, ON THEIR 1953-1954 BRITISH TOUR.

WILSON, KEPPEL AND Betty, Max Bygraves, David Whitfield and Vic Oliver and Johnny Duncan And His Blue Grass Boys.... Johnny Duncan was an American serviceman, I say to the Edinburgh Festival Theatre's David Montgomery. Cleaned up in Britain with 'Last Train To San Fernando'. There just weren't any American rockers around to play the halls in the late 1950s. But I preferred the Billy Connolly version, 'Last Train To Glasgow Central', it was early 1970s, from when he was not, painfully, the comedy king loved by millions.

When the going was old: Laurel and Hardy in Scotland in 1954.

David Montgomery doesn't know either version. He is showing me the wall down from level three of the Festival Theatre, covered with pictures of stars whose lights went out when The Beatles docked from Hamburg. And there is an original silk programme from November 7 1892, when Frank Matcham's new theatre, the first Moss Empire, opened. It featured a "grand sketch fantasia" and starred Miss Katy Cohen, Mr Ben Nathan, Miss Judah Warwick, Mr Harry Atkinson, Miss Cora Stewart, Mr Albert Christian — and the Cragges. The Cragges. I think about it, an inscrutable Scottish act. Jugglers? Acrobats? A family affair? Midlothian's Masters Of Mirth?

Matcham came back in 1910 to restore the Edinburgh Empire after a lethal fire. But then, in 1928, just before their Southampton Empire opened, Matcham's nemesis, W. and T.R. Milburn arrived. The old Empire was demolished, apart from a small part of the left-hand wall, and what is arguably the Milburns' masterpiece went up in its place. Great sight lines, closeness to the audience, and, after the last hurrah of variety in the 1950s, a long day's journey into bingo.

"Look at this picture," says David Montgomery. It is Princes Street, Edinburgh, with Scott Memorial, April 1954. It was at the time of Laurel and Hardy's last tour, and they weren't up to it. Their film career was washed up and they couldn't get a London West End booking — but they did play the Finsbury Park Empire. They had arrived in October 1953, 60-year-old "Oliver" Norvell Hardy of Harlem, Georgia, and 63-year-old Arthur Stanley Jefferson — the official name-change came in 1931 — late of Ulverston, Lancashire, and later of Beverley Hills, California.

The act that summed up the wondrous mysteries of mid-twentieth century British variety: Wilson, Keppel, and, of course, Betty.

"I mean," says David Montgomery. "Have you ever seen anything like it?"

There are Laurel and Hardy, and there is the crowd. Every citizen, every child of Edinburgh out to see the two men, one of whom had debuted on stage at the Britannia Theatre, Glagow in 1906, and the other, as "The Ton Of Jollity", at Cutie Pearce's Roadhouse, and at the Orpheum, in Jacksonville, Florida in 1913. I think of the Edinburgh crowd of 1954 as an extra, an homage, to vaudeville, variety, the 'Trail Of The Lonesome Pine' and The End.

The double act was due to finish the tour on May 24, 1954 in Swansea. But on May 18 Hardy suffered a heart attack in Plymouth. Their performance in the seaport on May 17 was their last anywhere. Hardy died in 1957, Laurel eight years later.

The Finsbury Park Empire closed in May 1960. Its last act was Emile Ford and the Checkmates, big that year in the hit parade with 'What Do You Want To Make Those Eyes at Me For?' a vaudeville hit from 1916, the year that Ollie Hardy made fifty-five Vim shorts in Florida. The Birmingham Empire was bombed in 1940, demolished in 1950. New Cross closed in 1956, Chiswick and Sheffield's Empires three years later, Leeds in 1961. In Cardiff, the Empire where Oswald Stoll had first flourished was demolished in 1962. The Glasgow Empire, where English acts died, died itself in 1963. Thirty years earlier, when Laurel and Hardy had visited that city, nine Glaswegians had been hospitalised in the welcoming riot at Glasgow Central Station.

The Holborn Empire, late Weston's, had a big sign up proclaiming "London's Real Music Hall" and it was the last theatre playing variety in the West End when the Luftwaffe blasted in 1941. One day in 2005, I went into the office low-rise that replaced it — a diminutive relative of the block that ousted the New York Empire — and asked about relics. "There were bits and pieces," said the doorman, pointing below, "until last year. Then they got rid of everything. I had some stuff, tried to get someone interested. No dice. Ended up on a skip."

Edinburgh didn't die. "Mecca Bingo unkindly got rid of every seat in the

The Holborn Empire was the last pure variety theatre in the West End, until, in 1941, the Blitz caught up with it.

stalls," says David Montgomery. "So the only original seats are in the Upper Circle. It has the second largest stage in Britain. It was the largest until Covent Garden got the extension."

The idea of turning the Empire into an opera house first came up in the mid-1970s. Two decades later the architects Law and Dunbar-Nasmith ripped out the old frontage, and put in a magnificent new façade of glass and light. They built a new stage house too, but the Milburns' magnificent auditorium was left. There is a lot of theatre space in Edinburgh, Festival aside, for a city of four hundred and fifty thousand people. The American conglomerate Clear Channel is down the road at the vast, ugly and lucrative Playhouse. The Festival is home to Scottish Opera and Scottish Ballet, but that week to David Essex in *Boogie Nights*.

"My idea of a good theatre is one that has a bum on every seat," says David Montgomery. We are on stage, looking out at two thousand vacant Festival Theatre tip-ups. "I have grown to love this place," he says. We keep on looking. "Some people are behind a computer from nine to five. But here, every now and again, if I have had a bad day, and there is no-one in, I just come in, lift the curtain and stand here."

Edward Moss and Richard Thornton bought up the old Alexandra Theatre in Liverpool in 1895. Frank Matcham got to work and by 1896, the Liverpool Empire had opened. Twenty-nine years later the Milburns arrived. Their Liverpool Empire was the first of that last wave of Moss Empires, a wave that, having finally ebbed in the 1970s, meant that it was bought by Merseyside County Council in 1979.

"When I came here," says the Liverpool Empire's "outreach officer" Sue Newall, "it wasn't Clear Channel, it was Apollo Leisure."

We are in her office on a late winter afternoon. It is in the heights of the theatre, crammed with *Bombay Dreams* costumes she made for the kids' production she is putting on. I am late; I parked at the top of the high-rise car park at Lime House Station. "Is the Empire next door?" I ask the attendant. He looks worried. No he says, wrong Lime Street. It is across town. Miles away. I swear. He laughs, points across the street at the Liverpool Empire. Scouse humour, can't beat it. I take the lift, on the dimpled metal is a critique scrawled in Dayglo, of the former Everton football star, gone for Manchester United. "Wayne Rooney is Judas", it says.

I do not know Liverpool. The Empire is part of a complex of the buildings — what is now labelled the cultural quarter — the city built on the back of

the trade of the Atlantic rim. In the dusk, the Empire with the Walker Art Gallery, St. George's Hall, the boulevards, the grass and the crowds pushing into the Empire is Imperial Rome on a good night with electric lighting and golden blue-grey sunset over the Mersey. The theatre glows, its old exterior wall is now part of a huge new space, out of the monied late twentieth century, glass, white wine, white stone, receptions — you're such a lovely audience we'd like to take you home with us. "The last time The Beatles played Liverpool," says Sue Newall, "was December 5 1965. And it was here."

Sue Newall is from Birmingham. "Liverpool," she says. "is great, architecturally amazing. I live in the Georgian quarter and the buildings are fantastic, more Georgian buildings than Bath. All built on the slave trade of course."

"So," I ask, "what is the difference between Clear Channel, and Apollo Leisure?"

"There isn't much difference. Clear Channel is just bigger."

Another persisting success from the Milburns' architectural era, the Liverpool Empire.

Much bigger. Where once there was Moss Empires and Keith-Albee, there is now Clear Channel, out of San Antonio Texas. The world's largest provider of live entertainment, plus 1,500 radio stations and 37 television stations. In Britain it owns, or operates, 23 theatres, and produces shows like *Miss Saigon*, *The King And I*, and *Chicago*. In the United States it has been slammed for right-wing bias. The internet offers a Clear Channel Sucks website.

That week at the Liverpool Empire, Clear Channel hosts another US conglomerate, the Disney Corporation, and its touring *Winnie-the-Pooh*. Across the auditorium, under the arches and spans of a Milburn masterpiece the matinee is packed. "Disney has brought its own booster seats to make them higher for little kids, so they can see," says Sue Newall. "Everything is covered." She laughs. "It is just their bankrupt parents who will be disgruntled. The show this week is sold out. For every performance."

There is a Liverpool great and good board of trustees. "They have the power to say we don't want that show brought in," says Sue Newall. Lottery money and Euro-money and Foundation for Sports and Arts money went in before Clear Channel.

She works with children, teenagers, old people; people are proud of the Empire, she says, and nowadays there is nothing that can't be staged. Sometimes with five- or six-year-olds, they get confused between cinema and theatre. "They know you need costumes and lights, and they know it's dark and they have tipping up seats. But sometimes grasping that the show is live, that's what they are surprised about, that there are people actually up there, performing." But they remember, and, on the backstage tours for old people, there will always be at least one adult who takes her aside and says "I remember coming here as a child".

She organises sessions for older school kids who say they don't want to do it, sometimes, and in the end, say it was great. Very, very occasionally she comes across certain kids who have potential — if she can meet the parents, and just talk. "Last February," she says, "We did *Copacabana*. We had a girl, she had never been before, we cast her as the lead girl, Lola. She had only been dancing for a couple of years. She was 15. She had only got into dancing at school, not from the age of five and always went to Saturday morning dance class. The school careers people had told her not to get into dancing as a profession. 'Do something sensible,' they told her.'"

Sue Newall and Amy, the Empire's dance teacher, told her to ignore the school's advice.

"There are lots of things you can do with dance," says Sue Newall. "And she is bright too and stunning-looking and has the figure for it — which in this kind of theatre is important — she now comes to our Tuesday night dance class and John Moores University do a great dance degree."

Ranged Empires fall

Let Rome in Tiber melt, and the wide arch
Of the ranged empires fall. Here is my space
Kingdoms are clay.

WILLIAM SHAKESPEARE'S *ANTHONY AND CLEOPATRA*, ACT ONE, SCENE ONE.

A fight with the elements: The Empire Grand Forks was born into a blizzard, reborn after a flood and a fire.

IN CINCINNATI, OHIO there was, once, a plan for its fine, old, quite derelict Empire on Vine Street. In June 2002, a local sporting star, announcing that he was "ready to go" and wanting to "put a hard hat on and start hitting some of this stuff", launched a plan to restore the 1909 Empire as a night club, backed by one hundred and eighty thousand dollars of local authority money. Alas, the star decamped, with the cash, and the roof of the theatre fell in. He was later convicted on seven theft-related charges, and given four years. The wide arch — and everything else — of that Imperial has now fallen. There is now only space, and Cincinnati clay.

Other Empires and Imperials fared better. Augusta Georgia got behind its Imperial as an arts facility. In San Antonio the Empire, which opened in 1913 as a vaudeville house, became a cinema, and closed in 1978. A decade later the City of San Antonio bought the theatre. Two decades later, as the Charline McCombs Empire Theatre, it reopened. And then there is the Empire of Grand Forks.

"It was not, of course, always an Empire," says the Empire, Grand Forks' Mark Landa. "But it has been an Empire for fifty years. It opened as the Grand, a movie house, in 1919. In a blizzard."

Grand Forks, North Dakota, where the Red River meets the Red Lake River, seventy-five miles south of Canada —Manitoba and Saskatchewan — with Minnesota just to the east; and beyond the Bad Lands, far to the west, Montana; and, to the south — South Dakota. The state of North Dakota, incorporated into the Union in 1889, state capital Bismarck. Dakotans thought that a capital named after Iron Chancellor Otto von Bismarck might just entice Teutonic investment on to the open midwestern plains.

Population of North Dakota, just under one million, and of Grand Forks, fifty thousand. "It is a typical midwestern town, an agricultural centre," says Mark Landa. "But there are another one hundred thousand people within thirty miles."

There had been another Grand Theatre nearby, but during the First World War it was wrecked by fire. Once that, too, had been an Empire, but when it reopened as a vaudeville house, as part of the all-powerful Keith-Orpheum chain, it became the Orpheum. In 1930 the Grand became the Paramount.

Inside Grand Forks, and in search of the past...

And a quarter of a century after that, into the world of padded shoulders, wide screens, plaid jackets, colour and Cinemascope, it became the Empire. Why? Because the state had become an empire within a union that had become the greatest power in the history of the planet.

"It was renamed at a time in North Dakota," says Mark Landa "when oil was discovered, there was mining, coal, it was that confident time postwar, farming — farming was still growing."

Along with minerals and wheat, there was Cold War. In the mid-1950s, fifteen miles out of town they started digging the Grand Forks Air Force Base. In the years that followed, so did the Voodos, the DeltaDarts, and the B52s. In 1966 the deployment of Minuteman missiles began. Amidst the sea of cereals, stretching beyond the horizon, silos were sunk with the capacity to unleash planetary extinction. Then the Soviet Empire crashed. The last bombers left Grand Forks in 1994. In April 1994 the Empire cinema closed down, there were multiplexes and shopping malls and the Empire's equipment was too old anyway. "The missiles went from the air base 15 years ago," says Mark Landa. "Now it is just KC135 tankers."

In December 1994 the owners of the Empire donated it to the local arts council. "The place was set up as it is by several business leaders and people in the arts, there was a teacher of education at the University of North Dakota in Grand Forks and her husband, who runs liquor stores and motels," says Mark Landa. "There was some local resistance but not much — it was mainly private money anyway."

The rebuilding as an arts centre began in late 1995, scheduled for completion in September 1997, but before that there was an art exhibition and a cabaret singer from over the state border in Minneapolis, concerts and a return showing for Buster Keaton's *The General* after sixty-eight years.

In a place of cruel winters, the winter of 1996-1997 was very bad, mountains of snow. With the spring thaw came the worst flooding in North Dakota's recorded history. "The remodelling was going on," says Mark Landa, "and we had that major flood. And then, at the same time, there was a fire. We are still paying the money from all that back."

Yet the Empire recovered. Mark Landa joined it early in the twenty-first century. "The group who were running it," he says, "were not experienced in running a business. They had big plans, and six full-timers, but they didn't know how to run an arts centre. I had never run an arts centre but I did know how to run a business and it was hard for me to fail, because everyone else had failed already, so all I could do was the same, or do better. I did better. And it is the most unique job I have ever had."

The theatre is Downtown, where Grand Forks started back in the 1870s. Most of retail business has moved out, so it is an area of small shops, restaurants, apartments.

"A lot of the older residents," says Mark Landa, "know the Empire because it is where they saw their first movie and it has a décor which tries to capture the early days. People are just proud of the place. I get a buzz from the Empire. I get a buzz every time the lights are turned on. We really know that we are a community theatre, where people think it is a treat to come over and perform on a real stage, in a real theatre."

Nowadays it plays amateurs and professionals and the Grand Forks Symphony Orchestra gets respectable audiences. The military does come to shows, but not as much as Mark Landa would like. By mid-2005 locals were worried the base would close and take jobs with it.

The North Ireland Territorial Army Band were invited by the North Dakota National Guard and worked through The Beatles and swing, and bagpipe music, and Bo Diddley packed the Empire out in 2004, playing for two hours and spending an hour signing autographs. "It was a great show," says Mark Landa, "my favourite. Showed what we were capable of doing. He was a great guy, he had a great time and we made money on the deal."

In 1912 and 1916 North Dakota went for Woodrow Wilson, in 1932 and 1936 for Franklin D. Roosevelt, and in 1964 for Lyndon B. Johnson, otherwise the state votes Republican. "North Dakota," says Mark Landa, "is very conservative. Grand Forks is conservative, but not quite so conservative. I don't try to push the limits too often."

The Empire did put on *The Vagina Monologues*. And there was a North Dakota spoof documentary movie about two stock, folkloric mid-western Scandinavian characters, Ole and Lena. The kids liked it, says Mark Landa. "Older people — they just hated it.

"The worst thing," he goes on, "was probably a local group who put on a Shakespeare festival. But what they didn't do was a Shakespeare play. They should have done, people would have known what they were expecting. What they did was scenes from Shakespeare; for four or five hours. They started with about one hundred and fifty people, but people would, I guess, slip out. There were about fifty at the end. The group thought that we needed Shakespeare in Grand Forks. But if they haven't killed Shakespeare in Grand Forks, I don't know what will."

America is ungovernable

As the great Liberator Bolivar had said in the bitterness of his spirit, "America is ungovernable. Those who worked for her independence have ploughed the sea".

NOSTROMO, BY JOSEPH CONRAD (1904).

SEVENTY YEARS AGO Caracas was a quiet colonial town nestling in a valley under the wonderful Mount Avila, an afterthought in the Andean chain. Even Caracas's most famous son, Simon Bolivar, El Libertador, might still have recognised it, and he had been dead since 1830. Then, half a century ago, Venezuela's postwar dictator, Perez Jimenez, imposed the modern world, ripping down houses, and slashing motorways across the capital, while shanty towns crept up the valley's lower slopes.

But those were boom times. Venezuela was, is, an oil superpower. Migrants flooded in from Portugal, Spain, Italy and from elsewhere in Latin America. A little area of west Caracas, popular with Canary Islands immigrants, took its name from them, La Candelaria.

One overcast humid day in Caracas I head west, under vast sky, along the urban autoroute, past billboards for Scotch and cigarettes and El Presidente, Venezuela's ever-present president, Hugo Chavez. Off the motorway the ride towards Avenida Urdaneta is into agreeable chaos, tight, narrow, jammed streets, people, noise, making out, slivers of sky; then La Plaza La Candelaria, Senora Nelly B. Lugo de Perez, and her Teatro Imperial.

It was her father-in-law who built it, she says, in her upstairs office. Oscar Ochao Palacios, dead in 1994 at 93, a man who lived the Venezuelan century from agrarian backwater to land of the Sauditos — the Saudis — as Venezuela's jealous neighbours, the Colombians, called them. Ochao Palacios was one of those creating infrastructure for modern Caracas. "He took a piece of land," says Senora Lugo, "drew in the roads, sold plots, five Bolivars a metre; payment, five Bolivars a week." Ochao Palacios built entire neighbourhoods in the east and west of the city, some of the biggest developments in all Latin America.

Senora Lugo is uncertain if the Teatro began with theatre. "It was built in the 1950s, and it was one of the first luxurious cinemas of those times." Senora Lugo is pensive. "Above the cinema, there were apartments, the whole building was apartments. In those early days the area was good immigrant people from Spain, but then it deteriorated..."

So did the movie business. In the mid-1970s it became two cinemas. In 1989 the cinema closed, the apartments became offices; the balcony became

Nelly B. Lugo de Perez of the Imperial.

the basis of the Teatro Imperial Centro de Convenciones, a meeting hall-cum-convention centre-cum art gallery. The main auditorium became — a parking lot.

We take the lift down. Lots of people have used the meeting hall, says Natalia Arias, a Colombian immigrant from the late 1980s. "There are religious gatherings, school graduations. — I like watching children getting diplomas and medals," she smiles, "folk dancing. Christians, some of them are strange but the Christian Mission, that is not bad."

"The Moonies hired it six years ago, but the Church got them out of the country," says Senora Lugo. "I let charities have it free, like the Alzheimer's people." We descend below the meeting hall into the auditorium/car park big, covered, still unmistakeably cinema. A concreted office, behind where the screen would have been, leaping technologies, has become an internet café. "Children come to do their homework, seven days a week," she says. "People wanted to have rave parties here, but I said no."

In the late 1990s someone else arrived. Venezuela, a democracy since Perez Jimenez was overthrown in 1958, was racked by corruption scandals. A young army colonel, who had been jailed after an abortive coup he had led in 1992 began holding meetings in the Teatro Imperial. Senora Lugo gestures upwards. "That is where the workshops for the constitutional assembly took place," she says. "This was a place for the launching of Colonel Hugo Chavez." In those days, she goes on, she supported Chavez. She laughs. "Later all the anti-Chavistas met here. Since the coming of Chavez many people are fearful of coming to this part of town because of confrontations, so our art gallery had to stop."

I edge along the perimeter of the old cinema, old signs are still visible. The walls have been decorated with paintings of houses. Senora Lugo's husband got a Candelaria artist to do the work. It is great, gorgeous, I tell her.

A smile flits across her face. "Good, huh? But then they are like Chavez. Behind, there is nothing."

The world was modern, and movies made in Rome were big in Caracas. Teatro Imperial de Caracas, Venezuela in 1962.

A moving tale of Empire

LONG BEFORE JIM Bailey and RuPaul in the United States, and Danny La Rue in Great Britain, there was Julian Eltinge of Newtonville, Massachusetts. And Eltinge was one of the most famous female impersonators of all time. The gowns and the singing were acclaimed, and, in the pre-First World War era, he pioneered celebrity own brands, marketing the *Julian Eltinge Magazine And Beauty Hints* and his own fashion lines.

Eltinge put on — and took off — weight in his later years but in his youth he transformed himself, with the help of his male Japanese dresser Shima, into splendid Gibson Girls, brides, and bathing beauties, developed Spanish, Asian and Salome dance routines and was hailed as true art. The key to his act was respectability; the bedrock of his following was amongst middle class housewives. The show business weekly *Variety* proclaimed that "Eltinge's act is extremely high class".

Born in 1883, the son of a mining engineer, William Dalton, as he then was, spent much of his early life in California. Back on the East Coast, in Boston, in the 1890s, he was the centrepiece of the First Corps Cadets' annual revue. By 1904 Dalton had become Eltinge and he gravitated from amateur productions to feature in *Mr. Wix Of Wickham* in New York, which,

144

despite having music by Jerome Kern, flopped. But Eltinge didn't. He switched to vaudeville and, at the age of twenty-three, was playing London, Paris, Vienna and Berlin.

In 1911 he featured in *The Fascinating Widow* at New York's Liberty Theatre. This musical comedy had a book by Otto Harbach — who gave the world *No No Nanette* and *The Desert Song* — and what became, in Eltinge vehicles, a familiar plot line — young man forced to dress as a woman to escape pursuers, in this case a detective. The show only lasted seven weeks in New York but its producer, A. H. "Al" Woods, put *The Fascinating Widow* on tour — and made a lot of money. Woods was impressed with Eltinge.

So impressed was he that in 1912, when Woods opened his own 880-seat theatre, designed by the great American theatre architect Thomas W. Lamb, Woods said to Eltinge: "Sweetheart, you're a big money-maker for me, and I am going to name my theatre for you." Thus was the Eltinge born. It launched with a melodrama, *Within The Law*, which ran for what turned out to be the theatre's record run, of 541 performances.

Eltinge was to play in plenty more of Woods's productions, and his career flourished into the 1920s. He began appearing in films from around 1917 — even making an appearance in an early Rudolph Valentino movie — and set up his own Julian Eltinge Players who toured vaudeville theatres.

After the ball was over came the Burlesque: the Eltinge in 1932.

Eltinge's sales pitch over an act, which inevitably triggered opposition from bigots and moralisers, was encapsulated in a piece in the *New York Dramatic Mirror* in 1921. This said that he was outstanding in vaudeville, "the peer of his class, the manliest man off-stage and the girliest girl on-stage". A Tin Pan Alley insider Gilbert Dean said, "As a 'she' he was glorious to look at. Yet he was known to have beaten up many a tough longshoreman and hoodlum. I know he was truly a 'he-man'. Don't ask me how — I know." Indeed, it may be best not to ask. Other unkindly insiders suggested that Eltinge's press agent had hired the longshoremen to stand around in a Ninth Avenue bar, attack Eltinge, and get beaten up.

By the late 1920s the best days were over for Eltinge, and for his theatre on 42nd Street, where Al Woods's last big hit was *Black Birds Of 1928*. Out in California Eltinge played himself in a bad talkie in 1931 but there were no more New York stage appearances between 1927 and his swansong in 1940.

Yet the Eltinge Theatre hung on. There were plays by the likes of Arnold Ridley and Preston Sturges in the 1920s, but, later, came burlesque and strippers. On March 7 1941 Eltinge died in New York, nine months later came Pearl Harbor and the following year the Eltinge closed, to reopen as the Laff Movie, largely showing comedies and cartoons. Then, renamed the Empire, from 1954 to its closure in the mid-1980s, the old theatre was a second-run movie house. Like the 42nd Street around it, the once proud Eltinge slid into decay. Yet what remained unchanged, unlike the

repertoire, were Lamb's magnificent
Edwardian façade, more or less intact and a
mutilated, but surviving auditorium.

Then, as the twentieth century ended, and
with the multi-billion dollar moves to
revitalise the Times Square–42nd Street area,
attention refocused on the Empire. And just
like Julian Eltinge himself, nothing was to be
quite as it seemed. The owners, the AMC
corporation, decided to move the façade of
Lamb's theatre two hundred feet, from 236
West 42nd Street, to 234 West 42nd Street,
which is what happened on March 1 1998.
And so in April 2000 the Eltinge, which had
turned itself into the Empire, turned itself
into the relocated AMC Empire 25, and
reopened as a 25-screen multiplex with
almost 5000 seats.

Which is where, a few years on, I finally
catch up with Woods's beautiful little theatre,
at a point when I almost think I know the
place. There is something of the Stepford
Wives about Empire 25. High above that
beautiful Teddy Roosevelt-era façade, is a
vast, sterile high-rise. But then Eltinge was good at putting up façades himself.

That day there are queues for the movies, all twenty-five of them, which
would have cheered Al Woods. And then there is the auditorium, grey-tiled
floor, brick-coloured paint and cream marble. Two balconies which look like,
must be, the originals and then there is the proscenium, which framed *Within
The Law*, with its three Edwardian nymphs dancing to Pan's flute. Between
them, twenty-first century escalators pump customers into the heart of
cinematic darkness. "I never used to come here," a nice old lady sitting under
the marble tells me. I ask why. "There was nothing clean, nothing respectable.
All pornography." We stare at the nymphs.

I step back into the 42nd Street of the Easy Internet café, Universal News,
Applebees, Hilton Times Square, Modells Sporting Goods— and a Madame
Tussauds. It has, I understand, a wax model of RuPaul — but not, I think, of
Julian Eltinge...

Only in America (II):
1917 and male
impersonator Julian
Eltinge arrives at
Hollywood's Lasky
Studios to make his
film debut and a
photo-call, with 25-
year-old child
impersonator Mary
Pickford.

Somehow still about

Oh! it really is a werry pretty garden,
And Chingford to the eastward could be seen;
Wiv a ladder and some glasses,
You could see to 'Ackney marshes,
If it wasn't for the 'ouses in between.

'IF IT WASN'T FOR THE 'OUSES IN BETWEEN', TUNE BY GEORGE LE BRUNN, LYRICS BY EDGAR BATEMAN, SUNG BY GUS ELEN (1899).

A songsheet for Hackney... Gus Elen and 'The 'ouses in between'.

(*Right*) Frank Matcham's blueprint for a dream: original architectural sketches for the Hackney Empire.

SOMETIME IN THE late 1980s I went to a talk at the Hackney Literary and Philosophical Society. The Society, a Victorian creation redolent of self-improvement, help and creativity — having expired early in the twentieth century had been revived by a group which included a friend of mine, a socialist doctor working in the East End, David Widgery.

The Society met in a pub down the road from the Hackney Empire. That evening the subject was Does Hackney Make People Mad, Or Do Mad People Move To Hackney? The main address was given by a local mental health expert. He said, as I recall, that the area had been a thriving centre for lunatic asylums in the eighteenth century. One was run by a Mr Barme and one by a Mr Batty. He suggested — although the Oxford English Dictionary offers no confirmation — that this could have been the origin of the terms used to define eccentricity or madness. He pointed out that Hackney is indeed a very deprived area of London, and this had an impact on the level of mental illness. He also suggested that there was some anecdotal evidence that mad people did move to Hackney. For them, or for their grateful or relieved relatives urging them on, it seemed the right place to be.

I lived for a decade in Hackney. It is indeed an eccentric place, but then, in their way, so are Grand Forks North Dakota, the South Bronx and La Candelaria, Caracas. Hackney is noisy, grim, peaceful, scary, ridiculous, accident-prone, exciting, haphazard. During the Second World War other parts of London were hit by more V1 flying bombs and V2 rockets, but Hackney got there first as a target. What better place to randomly drop in on than Grove Road London E4, on June 13, 1944, at twenty-five past four in the morning?

Hackney has, it says, more artists per acre than anywhere else in Europe. It has a spectacular racial mixture. Eighty-nine languages are spoken in its schools; there are Somalis, Turks, Vietnamese — in the long shadow of the

Back then... This was the beginning of the initial restoration in the 1980s.

Empire are a cluster of Vietnamese restaurants — Indians, Kurds, Chinese ... The Hassidim of Stamford Hill in Hackney comprises, it is also said, the largest Jewish community in Europe and the world's third largest after Israel and New York. What need of the diversity of lost global Empires when there is Hackney, and its Empire?

After raising more than £14 million, assorted disasters, the original building contractors going bust and more than two years — longer than it took to build back in 1901 — the Hackney Empire reopened, refurbished, on January 28 2004. The grand opening took place on the night of a rare London blizzard, with traffic sliding on snow-dusted white ice.

That night featured the Russian clown Slava Polunin and his Snow Show. Polunin was accompanied by a small troupe of clowns who, like him, provided finely focused visions of inscrutability and bewilderment. They were as one. Polunin's mime narrative nuzzled, shuffled, leapt around archetypes and the human condition and slid into the subconsciousness of the audience — or at least into mine. Back I went in my mystery train; Marcel Marceau, Beckett, Grock — I can only acknowledge him, not know him — Laurel and Hardy, Chaplin, Keaton, Weber and Fields, pantomime, *commedia del arte*, back towards that lustrous glow.

Polunin escaped a hanging, transformed himself into a steam locomotive, propelled globes into space, and, at the climax and conclusion, dematerialised inside a snowstorm. This billowed out, beyond the Empire's proscenium arch, swirled over the front stalls, the mid-stalls and the exit signs. The Russian's dreams engulfed us. In the Empire's auditorium children, grown-ups, punched Polunin's globes into the gold, red light and velvet darkness.

As a kid the Hackney Empire's Roland Muldoon had put variety shows on in the Guides' hut on his council estate in Weybridge, in Surrey. The first time he remembers seeing the Hackney Empire was in the 1970s.

We are sitting in his office. Walking across the Hackney Town Hall square that sunlit morning, I realise that I have rarely, recently, seen the theatre by day. It is magnificent. The brick glows.

"I was visiting a friend," he says. "Over the road. Oh look, I thought, a theatre, this really ugly old building with some kind of sign on it. And I didn't like the red brick frontage. There was buddleia peaking out of the cracks in the plasterwork and it was dingy looking, weatherworn. There seemed to be millions of birds living in it. And then there were the drainpipes; they were broken, so it was a drainpipe-stained building, without any real feeling. And an old-fashioned exterior."

In those days Claire and Roland Muldoon were the driving force behind CAST, the Cartoon Archetypal Slogan Theatre, born of the mid-1960s radical wave. The Hackney Empire, meanwhile, had expired as a variety theatre. There had been a spell when a commercial television company had taken over the place, then it became a bingo hall. John F Kennedy, Elvis Presley, Charlie Chaplin, Nikita Khrushchev, Harold Wilson, The Beatles, Charles de Gaulle, Ho Chi Minh, Lyndon Johnson, Willy Brandt, Richard Nixon, James Callaghan, and Jimmy Carter came and went and then it was the early-1980s. There was Ronald Reagan and Margaret Thatcher.

CAST was still touring. Mrs Thatcher was abolishing the metropolis's local government, the Greater London Council, because it was left-wing. The Arts Council of Great Britain, which had backed CAST was increasingly tepid, a polite word, about left-wing theatre groups. But CAST had set up a project, New Variety, in 1981 which had developed a circuit around London.

"We were," says Roland Muldoon, "quite into turns. Don't get me wrong. I always knew we lived in a different age. Lennie Bruce was our inspiration.

"But we had toured the north of England and seen all these working men's clubs with all these awful shows and we thought we ought to have our own alternative new variety. We decided to get a billiard hall, something like that, as a venue and put on comedy. So we said to our administrator, see if you can find any billiard halls."

The administrator came back and told them he had found just the place, only it was the Hackney Empire, and "they" wanted them to have it.

"There are two theories," says Roland Muldoon. "The guy who was the estates manager of Mecca, which owned the Empire, might have seen us play Wood Green in north London, or Mecca was just so eager to get shot of it that anyone who rang up would have got it. I looked at the place and I

In the beginning... The opening of the Empire in 1901.

Hackney much preferred the more raucous and down to earth comedian.

CLARKSON ROSE RECALLING THAT EMPIRE IN *RED PLUSH AND GREASEPAINT* (1964).

151

Roland Muldoon, a key figure in the rebirth of the Hackney Empire: "We have a movement with us."

couldn't believe it. I ran away. Imagine! It was so big. And we were such a small theatre company."

When the group first visited, the staff refused them admission. They were not members of the bingo club. They enrolled, sneaked in, they weren't really sure. They wanted to see if they really wanted it. "While the bingo was going on," says Roland Muldoon, "there would be people, us, going round knocking walls. The staff became suspicious."

An issue was the Empire's crumbling terracotta domes; English Heritage insisted they had to be restored. At that stage the local council was sympathetic, came up with some money, the Muldoons put up their own property as a guarantee, there was other money, other ways and the theatre became a theatre again.

So Roland Muldoon finally got to get up on to the stage of the ugly old building with some kind of sign on it. "It was," he says, "love at first sight, a decade on. I have played in L-shaped rooms, in gymnasiums, at a miners' camp in Skegness, I have played everywhere, we deliberately went out of theatres to get a working-class audience, or an alternative audience. We always played in a proscenium-type position, got to one end of the room, and performed from there."

A "proscenium-type position" — I think about the Canterbury, respectably depicted in the 1850s; a row of lady and gentleman artistes, on a low platform-stage, staking out their own proscenium, performing for ranks

The way it was: how the top of the Empire looked, during restoration.

of jolly, sober fellows, seated at benches. I think about the reality of what would have been mid-nineteenth century bear-gardens, late twentieth century L-shaped rooms. Roll on the proscenium, and a sense of distance...

"I looked at the dynamic sight lines at the Empire that day," Roland Muldoon says, "and it was overwhelming, the most wonderfully focused stage I had ever seen. I thought, has it got anthrax this building? Why us? We got hold of it because it was in what they thought of as a dump, and there was no tube, no underground railway. They wouldn't have given it to us otherwise. There was a group of us, and that is what got us through. It was 1986, the darkest Thatcher hour, and we snatched this building and got audiences in because we have a movement with us."

Behind Roland Muldoon's shoulder, out of the big new plate glass window is Hackney Town Hall. Everybody I speak to about theatres has a thing about money. There is never enough, and it comes at the wrong time, with the wrong strings attached. That was what we were talking about at Empire meetings, across a decade, while I looked out of a shabby, leaking window in the darkness at Hackney Town Hall, and its often eccentric borough council.

I too was caught up in Hackney's accidental history, there by a tragic twist. In the 1980s David Widgery, fascinated by the East End, and by its history, campaigned for a resurgent Empire and co-wrote the Hackney Empire Preservation Trust's initial pamphlet. In 1992 David Widgery died,

No more the Hackney Empire
Shall find us in its stalls
When on the limelight crooner
The thankful curtain falls,
And soft electric lamplight
Reveals the gilded walls...

...I love you, oh my darling,
And what I can't make out
Is why since you have left me
I'm somehow still about

FROM JOHN BETJEMAN'S *THE COCKNEY AMORIST* (1966).

and his partner Juliet Ash — a fervent Empire campaigner — and I replaced him on the board.

The problems came, I think, after success, after the money, or some of it, was found. There was no such problem with the Cincinnati Empire because there was no success, just a four-year stretch for the luckless main protagonist. But when the guerrillas come down from the mountains, out of the desert, take over the city, then there are problems. But for that group in the mid-1980s there was hope.

"We took over this oasis," says Roland Muldoon, "with one palm tree and, all of a sudden, all these other caravans started to appear. We started to build up this independent oasis, opening the door to everyone we could think of. Our objective was a popular audience."

Forty per cent of the population of Hackney is from ethnic minorities. Twenty five per cent of the population is black, mainly black British, from an Afro-Caribbean background. One night at the Empire, transfixed, I sat through a routine from the black comedian Felix Dexter. It was very funny, but what I remember are the Nigerian jokes. The West Indian audience cracked up.

"Black audiences in Hackney were used in the 1980s to sitting in a church hall and watching Jamaican farces," says Roland Muldoon. "They weren't used to buying a ticket and getting an allocated seat. We had a political attitude, and the theatre was welcoming to black people. Looking at the waves of immigration that have come into London, my theory is that, when finally, a group of people become confident in their London-ness — Jews, Irish, Scottish — they put on their wave of variety, so the best variety shows, now, are black variety shows because of the ordinary audience that comes to it. Our objective was always a popular audience and the black audience presents to me the best working-class audience I have ever seen."

A coalition emerged around the Empire from the late 1980s. Radical comedians — brilliant good bad awful — took its stage. The Empire, continuing a CAST tradition from the 1960s, fly-posted London, aiming the Empire at anyone who would go — and there was an audience for an alternative. There was nowhere, says Roland Muldoon, for gay people to play. "Nowhere," he says, "that would welcome a lesbian choir."

There is a famous clip, he goes on, of a young woman leaving the Empire. The interviewer says: "How often do you go to the theatre?"

She says: "I never go to the theatre, this is the Hackney Empire."

Polunin, one-time young Soviet hero of clowning, first showed up at the

Empire in the late 1980s. Muldoon never forgot him, thinks he discovered him for the West, and delights in the finals of the new act of the year shows which light up the Empire, or John Hegley or Bill Hicks, dead in 1994 of cancer at 34, and, "wonderfully seditious". Wonderfully seditious and again the trade of the Atlantic rim, a Texan comedian washed ashore in London E8. The trade goes on. A decade ago I laughed, loudly, at a Scottish comic, then Bing Hitler. In Los Angeles Craig Ferguson now hosts CBS's *Late Late Show*, more post-Tony Pastor for American television.

"A century ago," says Roland Muldoon, "the jokes, I suppose, were pro-Empire. Now, post-miners' strike, post-feminism, post-poll tax, they are Green."

In that other century the Hackney Empire opened into the Boer War on Monday December 9 1901. Nineteen new smallpox cases had been reported in London that weekend; the Broadway star William Gillette was playing Sherlock Holmes for Charles Frohman at the Lyceum, and on the Hackney Empire bill, above the Bioscope animated photographs, was Miss Marie Kendall — grandmother of the 1950s movie star Kay Kendall — the Daineff Troupe of Girl Acrobats, and ninety years pre-Hicks, the Manhattan Comedy Four.

Topping the bill was "Joe Elvin and Co." Elvin, Soho-born, had refined

Slava Polunin, leaping around the human condition.

You don't want to get too romantic about it. What I remember is sitting up in the Circle surrounded by mounds of peanut shells.

THE WRITER JOHNNY SPEIGHT TO THE AUTHOR (1971).

155

his comedy act at Pastor's New Fourteenth Street Theatre on Union Square in New York City in the early 1880s. The Elvin persona was tough, lovable cockney hedonist, it was only lately that I discovered his catchphrase, chanted from the gallery of Hippodromes, Gaieties and the Hackney Empire, "I ain't barmy," they cried.

"I am still excited by the idea that the Hackney Empire, reborn, almost respectable, can still not be respectable," says Roland Muldoon. "There is still an edge to things."

'The boy I love', sang Marie Lloyd of Hoxton, 'is up in the gallery'. At her death they draped the beer taps in the Leicester Square bars with black, and one hundred thousand Londoners watched her funeral procession depart. One night early in 2005 I am up in the Hackney Empire gallery; the theatre, grand from the stalls, is spectacular from the gods. A Birmingham woman Moslem comedian is performing. She is good, but Shazia Mirza gets lost in the spot; I catch, fleetingly, the tiny figure of Lloyd, lost at the Empire, trick of the light.

Excited by the idea of the Hackney Empire; an audience of today, and Marie Lloyd of yesterday — and forever.

Picture acknowledgements

Every effort has been made by the publishers to contact copyright holders; however please contact the publishers if any omissions have been inadvertently made.

The publishers would like to thank the following for the use of pictures and illustrations — The Mayflower Theatre, Southampton; Hackney Empire; Sunderland Empire; Toowoomba Empire; Grand Forks Empire; The Imperial, St John, Canada.

AKG, London 113.
Bridgeman Art Library, London (www.bridgeman.co.uk) The Detroit Institute of Arts, USA, Gift of Dexter M. Ferry Jr 26.
British Museum 34.
Corbis UK Ltd. 27, 56 top left, 58, 70, 123, 15; /Bettmann 29, 54-55, 56 top right, 62, 63, 90, 122, 146 top, 147; /Blue Lantern Studio 96;

/National Gallery Collection; reproduced by kind permission of the Trustees of the National Gallery, London 18-19, /Fine Art Photographic Library 57, 67; /Gideon Mendel 155, 156; /John Springer Collection 77; /Jonathan Torgovnik 144,145; /Peter Aprahamian 8-9; /Philip de Bay/Historical Picture Archive 20, 21, 23; /The Mariner's Museum 92 top right.
Enrique Larez 142, 143.
Getty Images 6, 16, 28, 61, 64-65, 71, 72, 83 top left, 83 bottom right, 84, 86, 89, 91, 92 centre, 95, 97 top, 100, 105, 107, 111 top, 118, 136, 137; /Werner Wolff/Time Life Pictures 94.
Billie Love Historical Collection 102.
Mander & Mitchenson 39, 49, 109.
The Scotsman Publications Ltd. 134.
V & A Images/Theatre Museum 14 top left, 14 top right, 32, 37, 41, 42, 44, 45, 46 top, 46 bottom, 51, 81, 82, 87, 101, 103, 106, 111, 135, 148, 149.

BIBLIOGRAPHY

All places of publication London unless otherwise indicated.

American National Biography; General Editors John A. Garraty Mark C. Carnes, Oxford University Press (New York Oxford 1999)

American Metropolis: A History of New York City; George J. Lankevitch, New York University Press (New York 1998)

American Musical Theatre: A Chronicle Second Edition; Gerald Bordman, Oxford University Press (New York Oxford 1992)

The Australian Dictionary of National Biography Volume 8 1891-1939; General Editors Bede Nairn and Geoffrey Serle, Melbourne University Press (Melbourne 1981)

Blacking Up: The Minstrel Show In Nineteenth Century America; Robert C. Toll Oxford University Press (New York Oxford 1974)

Bright Lights Big City: London Entertained 1830-1950; Gavin Weightman, Collins & Brown (1992)

British Music Hall; Raymond Mander and Joe Mitchenson, Studio Vista (1965)

British Theatre In the 1890s; Edited by Richard Foulkes Cambridge University Press (Cambridge 1992) Chapter 7 Indecency and Vigilance in the music halls Tracey C Davis

Celebrating The Mayflower Southampton 75 Years; Paul Lewis, Southern Daily Echo (Southampton 2003)

The Cinemas Of South Tyneside; D. Johnson, (South Shields ISBN0946 406 235 undated)

The Collected Verse of G. Essex Evans; Angus & Robertson Ltd (Melbourne 1928)

Dan Leno; J. Hickory Wood, Methuen & Co (1905)

The Diary of Samuel Pepys M.A. F.R.S; Edited with additions by Henry B. Wheatley F.S.A, George Bell & Sons (1904)

Disraeli; Robert Blake, Eyre & Spottiswoode (1966)

Domestic Manners Of The Americans; Frances Trollope, New English Library George Routledge & Sons 1927 (1832)

The Early Doors; Harold Scott, Nicholson & Watson (1946)

Edmund Yates: His Recollections And Experiences; Edmund Yates, Richard Bentley & Son (1885)

Empires, Hippodromes & Palaces; Jack Read, The Alderman Press (1985)

Empire Theatre: Grand Forks North Dakota Christopher P. Jacobs (Internet)

An Encyclopaedia Of London; Edited by William Kent, revised by Godfrey Thompson, J.M. Dent & Sons Ltd (1970)

The Encyclopaedia Of New York City; Edited by Kenneth T. Jackson, Yale University Press New Haven & London The New York Historical Society (New York 1995)

The Faber Book Of London; Edited by A.N. Wilson, Faber & Faber (1993)

Frank Matcham: Theatre Architect; Edited by Brian Mercer Walker, Blackstaff Press (Belfast c1980)

The Fringes Of Power: Downing Street Diaries 1939-1955; John Colville, Weidenfeld & Nicolson (2004)

From The Bowery To Broadway; Armond Fields, Oxford University Press (New York Oxford 1993)

Gotham: A History Of New York City To 1898; Edwin G Burrows and Mike Wallace, Oxford University Press (New York Oxford 1999)

The Greatest Street In The World; Stephen Jenkins, G.P. Putnam's Sons (New York 1911)

The Great White Way: A Re-creation Of Broadway's Golden Era of Theatrical Entertainment; Allen Churchill, E.P. Dutton & Co Inc (New York 1962)

A Hard Act To Follow: A Music Hall Review; Peter Leslie, Paddington Press (1978)

The Historical Atlas Of New York City: A Visual Celebration of Nearly 400 Years Of New York City's History; Eric Homberger Alice Hudson (cartographic consultant), Henry Holt And Company (New York 1994)

The History Of American Theater: From Pre-Colombian Times To The Present; Felicia Hardison Londré and Daniel J Watermeier, Continuum (New York 1998)

A History Of London; Stephen Inwood, Papermac (2000)

Houdini: The Man Who Walked Through Walls; William Lindsay Gresham, Victor Gollancz (1960)

The House That Stoll Built; Felix Barker, Frederick Muller (1957)

The Illustrated Victorian Songbook; Aline Waites and Robin Hunter, Michael Joseph Ltd., (1984)

In the Nineties; John Stokes, Harvester Wheatsheaf (Hemel Hempstead 1989)

John Culme's Footlight Notes (Internet)

Last Days Of Knickerbocker Life In New York; Abram C Dayton, G.P. Putnam's Sons (New York 1897)

Laurel Before Hardy; Jenny Owen-Pawson & Bill Mouland, Westmorland Gazette (Kendal 1984)

Lost Broadway Theatres; Nicholas van Hoogstraten, Princeton Architectural Press (Princeton 1997)

London Labour And The London Poor; Henry Mayhew, Cass (1861-62)

London: The Biography; Peter Ackroyd, Chatto & Windus (2000)

Lost Empires; J.B. Priestley, Heinemann (1965)

Marie Lloyd: The One And Only; Midge Gillies, Victor Gollancz (1999)

Mrs Astor's New York: Money And Social Power In a Gilded Age; Eric Homberger, Yale University Press (New Haven London 2002)

Murray's Handbook Durham Northumberland, John Murray (1890)

Music Hall In Britain; D.F. Cheshire, David & Charles (Newton Abbot 1974)

My Autobiography; Charles Chaplin, Bodley Head (1964)

My Theatrical And Musical Recollections: Emily Soldene, Downey & Co Ltd. (1897)

The Newcomes; William Makepeace Thackeray, Smith Elder (1854)

A New History Of Jazz; Alyn Shipton, Continuum (London and New York 2001)

Ornamentalism: How The British Saw Their Empire; David Cannadine, Allen Lane The Penguin Press (2001)

The Oxford Companion To American Theatre Second Edition; Gerald Bordman, Oxford University Press (Oxford 1992)

The Oxford Companion To Canadian Theatre; Edited by Eugene Benson and L.W. Conolly Oxford University Press (Toronto Oxford 1989)

The Oxford Dictionary Of National Biography; Edited by H.C.G. Mathew and Brian Harrison, Oxford University Press (Oxford 2004)

Oxford Literary Guide To Australia; General Editor Peter Pierce, Oxford University Press (Melbourne 1987)

Penguin History of the United States Of America; Hugh Brogan, Penguin Books (1990)

Popular Culture & Class Conflict 1590-1914; Eileen Yeo & Stephen Yeo, Harvester Press (Brighton 1981)

Queen's Theatre South Shields website

Recollections Of Vesta Tilley; Lady de Frece, Hutchinson (1934)

Rediscovering Gandhi; Yogesh Chandha, Century (1997)

Red Plush And Greasepaint, Clarkson Rose; Museum Press (1964)

Rogue's Progress: The Autobiography Of "Lord Chief Baron" Nicholson; Edited by John L. Bradley, Longmans (First published 1860, 1965)

Ron Drew's Theatre Pages (Internet)

Saturday Evening Post (New York December 4 1948)

Scott Joplin And The Ragtime Era; Peter Gammond, Abacus (1975)

Selected Letters Of P.T. Barnum; Edited and introduced by A.H. Saxon, Colombia University Press (New York 1983)

A Short and Remarkable History of New York City; Jane Mushabac and Angela Wigan, Fordham University Press (New York 1999)

Siegfried Sassoon: A Study Of The War Poetry; Patrick Campbell, McFarland & Co (Jefferson North Carolina 1996)

Sixty Years' Stage Service: Being A Record Of The Life Of Charles Morton The Father of The Halls: Compiled by WH Morton & H Chance Newton, Gale & Polden (1905)

Sketches By Boz; Charles Dickens, Chapman & Hall (1898 first published 1868)

Sometimes Gladness: Collected Poems 1954-82 Revised Edition; Bruce Dawe, Longman Cheshire (Melbourne 1983)

Stan And Ollie; Simon Louvish, Faber And Faber (2001)

Stars Who Made The Halls; S. Theodore Felstead T. Werner Laurie (1946)

Sunderland Empire: A History Of The Theatre And Its Stars; Alistair Robinson, TUPS Books (Newcastle upon Tyne 2000)

Sweet Saturday Night; Colin MacInnes, MacGibbon & Kee (1967)

The Theatres Trust Guide To British Theatres 1750-1950; Edited by John Earl & Michael Sell, A&C Black (2000)

Vaudeville USA; John E DiMeglio, Bowling Green University Popular Press (Bowling Green Ohio 1973)

Victoria And Disraeli; Theo Aronson, Cassell (1977)

The Victorians; A.N. Wilson, Hutchinson (2002)

Victorian Entertainment; Alan Delgado, David & Charles (Newton Abbot 1971)

Victorian Spectacular Theatre 1850-1910; Michael R Booth, Routledge Kegan Paul (1981)

The Victorian Theatre 1792-1914: A Survey; George Rowell, Cambridge University Press (Cambridge 1978)

The Voice of the City: Vaudeville And Popular Culture In New York; Robert W Snyder (Oxford University Press (New York Oxford 1989)

The War Poems Of Siegfried Sassoon; Arranged and introduced by Rupert Hart-Davis, Faber & Faber (1983)

Where Dead Voices Gather; Nick Tosches, Jonathan Cape (2002)

Wink The Other Eye; Nicholas Morgan Patrick O'Connor Radio 3

Winkles And Champagne; M. Willson Disher, B.T. Batsford (1938)

World's End; Donald Wheal, Century (2005)